Penguin Education

Penguin Education Speci:
General Editor: Willem

GW00939177

The Special Child
Barbara Furneaux

Barbara Furneaux became interested in special
education after working for some time with normal
children. She has long been involved with the education
of slow learners and disturbed adolescents, and is now
Principal of The Lindens, a Surrey County Council unit
for severely disturbed, psychotic and autistic children.
She has published many articles on special education in
The Times Educational Supplement, *New Education* and
other journals.

The Special Child
The Education of Mentally Handicapped Children
Second Edition

Barbara Furneaux

Penguin Education

Penguin Education
A Division of Penguin Books Ltd,
Harmondsworth, Middlesex, England
Penguin Books Inc, 7110 Ambassador Road,
Baltimore, Md 21207, USA
Penguin Books Australia Ltd,
Ringwood, Victoria, Australia

First published 1969
Reprinted 1970
Second edition 1973
Copyright © Barbara Furneaux, 1969, 1973

Made and printed in Great Britain by
Hazell Watson & Viney Ltd,
Aylesbury, Bucks
Set in Monotype Plantin

This book is sold subject to the condition that
it shall not, by way of trade or otherwise, be lent,
re-sold, hired out, or otherwise circulated without
the publisher's prior consent in any form of
binding or cover other than that in which it is
published and without a similar condition
including this condition being imposed on the
subsequent purchaser

To the children and the parents

Contents

Note

All the opinions and views expressed in this book are personal ones of the author and do not necessarily reflect in any way the views of the local education authority by whom she is employed and which is not, therefore, in any way responsible for them.

Acknowledgements

There are many people to whom my thanks are due for the assistance they have given me in writing this book.

First there are the children themselves, in particular those whom I have in my care and from whom I constantly learn so much. There are also their parents, some of whom have freely given me their permission to quote from my experiences with their children. In order to preserve their privacy, in no case have I used the correct name of the child, and I have also, in some instances, made slight inessential alterations in their story to conceal further their identity.

My thanks are also due to: Dr N. O'Connor, Mrs W. A. Curzon, Dr L. Minski, Dr A. Kushlick, Miss E. Stephen, Miss J. Robertson, Miss R. Shakespeare, Mr Cummings, the National Society for Mentally Handicapped Children, the National Association for Mental Health, the Brighton Medical Officer of Health and the staff at the training centre and sheltered workshop.

My thanks are especially due to: Professor J. Tizard, Dr M. Rutter, Dr B. Kirman, Mr L. Bartak, Mr D. J. R. Morrison and Miss M. Johnson, who have been good enough to comment upon some of the separate chapters in this book as I prepared them.

My most particular thanks are due to my husband Professor W. D. Furneaux, without whose patience and tolerance I could not have found the time to write the book at all.

In preparing this second edition I have received invaluable help from the following:

Dr Kushlick, who has very kindly supplied me with a wealth of detailed information re the Wessex Experiment.

The heads of several junior training schools who have given up their time to give me their personal views of the consequence of the transfer of responsibility.

Mrs Partridge, Head Teacher of a large hospital training school.

Mr Evans, Mrs Mays, Mr Gregory and Mr Earl of the London Borough of Sutton.

To all of them and to the parents of the Leatherhead Branch of the National Society for Mentally Handicapped Children I would like to express my very sincere gratitude.

Part One
Introduction

'I am determined that these children shall take their rightful place in the educational system and receive their fair share of the resources available ... for there is no doubt that many of them can, with good care and training live useful and contented lives and can find satisfaction in gainful employment.' These words were spoken by Mrs Margaret Thatcher, the Secretary of State for Education and Science at a Regional Conference of the National Society for Mentally Handicapped Children in April 1971. The first of that month, April 1971, has historic importance for it was then that the Education (Handicapped Children) Act which had received the Royal Assent on 23 July 1970 took effect. In consequence, a hundred years after the passing of the Education Act of 1870 (which set out to establish a national system of education), universal compulsory education became a reality and the absolute right to full education for all children without any exceptions was legally established.

Who are these children – 'the last to come in' as the Report on Education no. 69 issued in March 1971 by the Department of Education and Science described them? To quote from the same report they are the children 'severely handicapped by reason of mental retardation' but who have 'many basic needs in common with ordinary children'.*

The acceptance of these children which this Act formalizes has relevance to the community as a whole, for apart from the immediate good it will bring to the children and their parents, it may have a wider effect in partly alleviating one of the most common anxieties of prospective parents as revealed by a survey reported on in 1966 by Miss Audrey Wood, General Secretary

* *Reports on Education*, March 1971, no. 69. 'The last to come in', issued by the Department of Education and Science, Curzon Street, London, W1Y 8AA.

of the Royal Society of Midwives. This comprehensive survey
was carried out in 1964–5 in London, Sheffield and Bristol; those
taking part were a cross-section of the normal communities of
the three cities, each representative of their own region. It seems
justifiable therefore, to assume that the anxieties it displayed are
widespread and common. It highlighted the well-known,
profound effect that a first baby has on the whole family situation,
and examined the attitude of the prospective parents, both
towards each other and to the expected baby. Interviews were
held with 1514 mothers of first babies, and the fathers took part
in group discussions. Two-thirds of the mothers had experienced
some kind of fear before pregnancy. The most common anxieties
were concerned with the birth itself and with the possibility of
having an abnormal child, especially one that was mentally
abnormal. The fathers had experienced similar anxieties but had
not discussed them at the time for fear of aggravating the
situation. During the term of the pregnancy this fear of having
an abnormal baby doubled, and it is interesting to note that
whereas only 17 per cent of the ante-natal sample admitted to
this, 62 per cent of the post-natal sample revealed that they had
had this dread.

Fortunately, for most parents, their fears prove to be
groundless, but nevertheless all the most recent surveys show
that in a standard population of 100,000 with a birth rate of
sixteen per 1000 per annum, one can expect to find ninety-six
severely sub-normal children aged up to fifteen. Taking the whole
of Britain, it appears that for every 1000 children between ten
and nineteen years old there will be 3·7 who are severely
subnormal. The usefulness of the concept of the Intelligence
Quotient (IQ) as a diagnostic measure will be discussed later in
the book. In these terms, however, severely subnormal means an
IQ as measured by a standard test, of 50 or under. (The average
IQ is 100). These are the worst affected: in addition there are
estimated to be 1·2 per cent whose IQs range from 50–70.

The parents of these children are the ones whose fears did
come true, who have to face the problem of accepting their
handicapped child: a problem which starts with the birth of the
child and which only too often is exacerbated by the reactions of
everyone else with whom the parents become involved, a problem

in which all too often they feel unsupported and rejected. The implementing of the new Act has now removed permanently some evidence of rejection and other measures which will be discussed later in this book should, as they become fully implemented, help to give more feeling of support.

The problem of educating and helping the mentally handicapped children of this country is an acute one, affecting a considerable percentage of the population. It appears to be hindered by many factors, one of the most potent of which seems to be the deep-rooted prejudices and fears not only of the public at large but also of many people who are actually involved in the work.

It is frequently said that the health of a nation can be judged by the care it takes of its less able and sick members. It is undoubtedly true that the Report of the Royal Commission on the Law Relating to Mental Illness and Mental Deficiency of 1957 and the subsequent Mental Health Act of 1959 supplemented in 1971 by the Department of Health and Social Security, *Better Services for the Mentally Handicapped* Command 4683, London HMSO reflect both the concern felt by the whole community and also the current widely-held ideas as to the proper and continuing care which should be freely given and easily available.

Nevertheless in 1967 at least one group of mothers asked, 'Our children are subnormal, must they also be treated as subhuman?' Describing the great difficulties she had had in obtaining any physical help for her subnormal child, one mother spoke on behalf of such children, as Shylock did for the Jew: 'if you prick us, do we not bleed; if you tickle us, do we not laugh; if you poison us, do we not die?' when discussing her longing and need for the support and aid of expert advice. She also said, 'Perhaps if I had been more incompetent I would have received some help.'

Even in 1972 a mother writing to *Parents Voice* the journal of the National Society for Mentally Handicapped Children described how 'For seven years I'd begged, pleaded, wept and nagged for this and other services for my severely subnormal son. Searching out assistance where I could, then persuading the appropriate authorities sometimes successfully, often not, to let him have the service.' She continues 'After seven years of banging my head against the proverbial "brick wall" I was offered – *offered*, help. How can I describe how I felt. I'd reached the top of the mountain and at last there was a view, a beautiful cheerful view.'*

This letter contains the whole essence both of the problem and the changing scene. Some parents are at last beginning to feel, to quote from the same letter again, 'There is light where before it was dull and grey and all is due to just a little bit of help'.

This book will attempt to examine and evaluate the help that is actually available for our mentally handicapped children. It has been necessary to divide this examination into three parts: firstly, the provisions for the severely subnormal and secondly, provision for the subnormal or slow-learners. The final section of the book examines the particular problems relating to those children who, although they appear subnormal, probably have a much higher intelligence level.

The first two chapters of the book serve as a general introduction to mental subnormality. Chapter one considers some of the causes and describes some types of mental subnormality. Chapter two presents the dilemma of parents with a subnormal child. All the cases are real but for obvious reasons, the names and in some cases, a few details have been changed.

* *Parents Voice*, Journal of the National Society for Mentally Handicapped Children, vol. 22, no. 2, June 1972, p. 16.

Chapter One
What is Mental Subnormality?

The child suffering from mental subnormality is not a species apart. There is no sharp distinction, no one crucial point which separates the normal person from the mentally retarded. The range of intelligence forms a continuum along which we all have a place and, although it is relatively easy to identify people at either extreme, it is not so simple to distinguish between the abilities of people who are near together on the continuum. Thus it is wrong to assume that the mentally subnormal are suffering from a single disease, namely the condition of subnormality. Rather, they are showing a symptom or symptoms of some impairment suffered during the course of their development. This impairment may be pathological, the consequence of disease, or due to cultural or social factors. Thus the mentally subnormal child is a potentially normal individual who has been damaged in some way, just as the deaf or blind child, and should be accorded the same concern, sympathy and positive approach we commonly show to the blind and the deaf. What is known about the causes of mental subnormality? The answer is, very little. There is evidence that pathological factors result in severer subnormality than social factors. But in general the nature and causes of retardation are obscure. Indeed, there is not even precise data on the incidence of subnormality. One main reason for this situation is the lack of money available for research. The Medical Research Council in all has funds which amount to less than 1 per cent of the expenditure of the Health Service.

However, the complexities involved in diagnosing and understanding subnormality are beginning to be realized. We are moving away from the dangerous absurdity of regarding as a homogeneous group all children who cannot reach an arbitrarily determined score on an intelligence test. Something of the nature of the problem can be illustrated by a series of studies of the admissions to the Fountain Hospital between 1955 and 1959. This hospital was then the main centre in London for mentally handicapped children. Of all children admitted, positive causes of subnormality could only be suggested for, on average, 20 per cent. This figure could probably be improved were a similar study to be undertaken today.

It is beyond the scope of this book to give a detailed and comprehensive discussion of this whole area, but I shall outline briefly some of the possible causes.

As mentioned earlier, the subnormal child has been damaged in some way and this damage could be due to genetic or environmental factors or both. One example of a genetically determined malfunction is the inherited chemical disorder known as phenylketonuria. Because of a faulty or missing enzyme, a child suffering from this is unable to assimilate properly an amino acid, phenylaline, which is present in our everyday diet. Instead, this substance is excreted in the urine. Since it is essential to normal brain activity, its absence leads to mental retardation of varying degrees. If the condition is quickly recognized in a new-born child it can be treated by a rigidly controlled diet.

Phenylketonuria is one condition that can cause two apparently normal parents to give birth to a mentally handicapped child. The parents do not suffer from it themselves but carry it as a recessive gene. As it does not affect the child until after birth, there is every hope that it can be recognized and averted.

There are other chemical disorders which result in the baby being abnormal at birth. In these cases relatively simple tests do exist to detect whether potential parents are carriers of these metabolic disorders. This is one area in which there is clearly need for research on preventive measures. It may be possible to reduce the incidence of these conditions if, as a matter of routine, all near relatives of known cases and their marriage partners were screened for the same condition. They could then be informed as to their chances of producing such an abnormal child.

Other inherited disorders which cause subnormality are related to the age of the parent at the time of the birth. The best known example of this is Downs' syndrome or, as it is commonly called, Mongolism. This condition is the result of a chromosome fault and the highest number of cases occur when the mother is over the age of thirty-seven at the time of the baby's birth. The incidence of this and other conditions of chromosome abnormalities could also be greatly reduced therefore if a chromosome investigation were to be carried out for all parents who for any reason might be considered to be 'at risk' of producing a baby with any form of chromosome disturbance.

Some malformations of the nervous system can be genetic in origin, but they may also be due to environmental causes. Here again there are many interesting hypotheses which need to be tested by controlled research. For example, there is evidence which suggests that an imperfect diet of the mother during pregnancy may be a cause of malformations and that the excess as well as the shortage of certain vitamins may be dangerous. If this were to be established, obviously the self-medication and over-prescription in 'developed' countries is as potentially dangerous as the shortages in underdeveloped countries.

There are other environmental causes which are relatively common and which may operate either before birth or at birth in the same way as the hereditary causes. The tragedy of the thalidomide babies is an example of environmentally caused damage which is well known to all, although of course, these babies are, on the whole, physically rather than mentally handicapped.

The Rhesus factor, a blood group incompatibility, results in a particular form of brain damage known as kernicterus, the second and later born babies being the ones 'at risk'.

Brain damage may also occur during birth and twin babies are particularly vulnerable to this – especially the second twin – who is more likely to suffer from lack of oxygen during the process. Some children suffering from cerebral palsy are mentally retarded and this form of damage to the brain may also occur at or about the time of birth. Babies born by breech delivery are more likely either to be still-born or to have some form of brain damage. Improvement in the provision of preventive obstetric care for all babies 'at risk' would reduce the incidence of mental retardation in all these cases.

A baby can be damaged after birth also – even apart from the risks caused by diseases such as meningitis and infantile paralysis. Blind children whose blindness is caused by an optic defect known as retrolental fibroplasia are a case in point, for this defect seems to be caused by an excess of oxygen being given to premature or low birth-weight babies.*

In some conditions both environmental and genetic factors may be important. Hydrocephalus and spina bifida are examples of this. These are cases of malformation of the nervous system in which the mother may have an inherited predisposition to have an abnormal child, which is increased by deficiencies in her own body at the time of pregnancy.

So far, some of the pathological conditions which may lead to mental and other forms of retardation have been discussed. Some of the less severe forms of retardation may be the product of social or cultural faults. Anything which adversely affects the health and care of the mother, before, during and after pregnancy may affect the baby. Defective housing conditions and poor feeding will operate in this way and their effect will continue after the baby is born. Since such an environment offers little in the form of necessary stimulus and few opportunities for activities which lead to healthy development, the effects will continue to operate progressively.

There is no evidence that the child of a mother with low intelligence will also be retarded to the same degree. In fact the contrary is true, for, on average, these babies will have a higher intelligence than their mothers. However, these mothers are more likely to live in the conditions traditionally associated with poverty and it is in consequence of this that their children sometimes function on lower levels than their intellectual potential would indicate. Illegitimate babies are 'at risk' in the same way for frequently their mothers lack proper pre-natal care and often have less favourable conditions for rearing their child. A realistic acceptance of the facts of illegitimacy by the community at large and the proper provision of facilities made easily available to the unmarried mother, such as are provided by some Scandinavian countries, would help to protect the intellectual potential of the child. We are rightly proud of the fact that progressive legislation has raised the standard of living and care for the people as a whole, but the fact that we have no room for complacency in

* Workers in premature-baby wards are now well aware of this danger and the chances of defect occurring are diminishing.

this respect and that the intellectual development of children is still being affected by bad environment was demonstrated by a pamphlet, *Back to School from a Holiday in the Slums* [1], which quotes some poignant examples.

For example, there is Marion, eight years old. She has one elder sister at school, one in the infants and two not yet at school. They live in cramped accommodation on the top floor of a big house. The children hardly ever sleep and are all nervy. Marion has to have four tranquillizers during the day and two at night. She is thin and pale and walks round in a dream. She clings to anyone who will take notice of her, which could prove highly dangerous one day (Headmaster of a Battersea primary school).

One four-year-old girl was admitted to the local nursery school unable to walk. The family lived in one room and their only form of heating was oil heaters. A neighbour's child had been badly burned when she knocked over a heater, so the mother of this girl kept her in her cot all day for safety! She was terrified that if she did not keep her daughter safe in this way, she would be burned too. The nursery school taught the girl to walk, with success. But now, two years later, she is more like a four-year-old than a six-year-old (Birmingham primary-school mistress).

Three-quarters of my children are deprived in some way or another. In 1966–7, 233 children were admitted into the school and during the year 172 pupils left – and this does not include those who left because they were going to a secondary school. The school is a transit camp for many of these children. The fact that they are in and out of this school is just another break in their schooling. It is nothing for a child of seven to have been to three previous schools since he was five (Headmaster of a Birmingham primary school).

What possible chance have such children of developing their full potential, particularly as this only indicates the fringe of the problems which they face? What kind of family relationships and security can develop in such circumstances? How can the parents provide even for their emotional needs and resolve their own problems in such conditions? Even if only a small number of children are affected, the situation would need urgent resolution, but in fact '1,420,000 children are living in over-crowded conditions'.

These then are some of the differing causes of mental subnormality. Although it is indisputable that even the experts are only now beginning to understand the problems involved, it is nevertheless true that the future prospects for reducing the incidence are good and improvements could be expedited if only the necessary resources were available. The crucial point is, of course, that so much depends upon the amount of money that can be devoted to preventive research. Even if the most pessimistically realistic view of the economy as a whole is taken, it still appears that there are some grounds for asserting that an unduly small amount is spent upon this problem. The task of the medical, educational and all the other services involved is not only to research into the causes and methods of reducing the incidence, but also to deal with the consequences. Diagnosis should lead to remedial measures being taken. These measures may be: therapeutic, such as the surgical improvement of conditions such as spina bifida or hydrocephalus; medical, as for example in the control of phenylketonuria; preventive, by means of such services as genetic counselling; or educational, which means the exploration of all possible means to improve the disabilities which are the inevitable consequence of the original defect. Many cases will need a combination of all these measures.

Chapter Two
Special Children and their Families

Jonathon is the second baby of healthy young parents. The birth of the first child was uncomplicated and as the mother's second pregnancy presented no problems, Jonathon was born at home. As soon as he was born, however, the midwife sent for the doctor who examined the baby and then immediately rushed him to hospital. The child was suffering from spina bifida; due to faulty development of the lower part of the spine, a section of the spinal cord, which carries vital nerves, was unprotected, and membranes were vulnerably placed just under the skin. An immediate operation improved his condition, but, nevertheless, as he grew, his parents learned that he was totally paralysed in the lower part of his body. He will never walk or have any control over his excretory functions. In addition, he also has a mild degree of hydrocephalus, which means that he is mentally retarded. Jonathon is a typical example of a child whose educational prospects will be radically altered by the new legislation. Even if, as he develops, his mental retardation is shown to be severe he will not be overlooked, for it is specifically stated in the relevant Circular 15/70 [1] sent out by the Department of Education and Science to all Local Education Authorities in September 1970 that from the date of the transfer of responsibility (i.e. 1 April 1971) 'No child within the age limits for education therefore, will be outside the scope of the educational system.' It is easy to imagine also the relief this provision will bring to his parents, both practically and emotionally. Previously they would inevitably have been told at some stage that he would never 'be suitable for education in school'.

In other cases there is no immediate sign of a physical malfunction, and not until the child is a few years old is aberrant behaviour apparent or extreme enough to justify fear of some underlying dysfunction. Like Jonathon's parents, Mr and Mrs

Martin are a normal, healthy couple. There is no history of mental illness in either of their families. Anne is their first child, and since they both wanted children, they were delighted when she was born. She was physically perfect and an attractive baby. Apart from the fact that she was rather difficult to feed – she never appeared to be hungry – her parents thought during her first year that they were extremely fortunate. Anne was so quiet and undemanding that 'no one knew we had a baby in the house'. She did not want to be picked up or cuddled, she never cried for attention, and as she was their first child, her parents did not think this was strange. She sat up at the right time, began to walk at the appropriate age. She continued to be quite undemanding which reinforced her parents' belief that they were unusually fortunate, although they were slightly concerned when she showed no signs of talking and hardly responded when spoken to. However, they had no other reason to suspect that she was deaf, and were reassured by the clinic doctor and the health visitor that children did vary a great deal in this way and so they should 'just wait and see'. Even this slight anxiety seemed to be unnecessary when just before her brother was born, Anne began to make babbling noises and some sounds which resembled speech. She went to stay with an aunt and appeared to be totally unaffected by the change. She stayed longer than was anticipated for the birth was delayed and it was also decided that since she was not upset and no trouble, she should not go home immediately after her mother had returned home with the baby. Once again she showed no sign of emotion when she did go home, but gradually her parents realized that she had stopped her attempts to speak and also that she was acting as if the baby did not exist. They also realized as the baby grew and they could compare his behaviour with Anne's, that there were many odd factors in her earlier apparent 'goodness'. Edward smiled responsively at them and when they approached him would put up his arms to be picked up and would also 'cuddle in'. Anne had never done any of these things. He wanted their company and stimulation and so, as he both demanded and responded to it, he got more of it from them. The mother began to feel that Anne and she had no point of contact. As she put it, she only existed for Anne as a useful machine to supply her with what she wanted when she wanted it. Her father got slightly more response from her as she would sometimes allow him to carry her or to have her on his knee.

When Anne was still not using speech at the age of four, the doctor did suspect that she might have some degree of deafness and so sent her for an audiological investigation. Although she did not respond in the normal way to any of the sound stimuli, the audiologist felt that there were indications that she was hearing, so referred her to a large children's hospital for a detailed neurological and physical investigation. She was still a very poor eater – in fact for eighteen months between the ages of two and a half and four years, Mrs Martin could not remember seeing her eat any solid food. She was very petite; at four she had the physique of an eighteen-month-old baby although her tiny frame appeared to be incredibly strong when she wanted either to manipulate her mother's hand to reach things for her or to retain possession of something which anyone wanted to take from her. Apart from her small size, however, the doctors could find no evidence of physical abnormality, nor of any physical reason for her lack of response to sound or to other external stimuli such as pain, nor for her failure to develop speech. She was therefore referred to the psychiatric department of the same hospital. She had her fifth birthday at about this time and at the request of the psychiatrist was admitted to school on a trial basis in spite of her lack of speech.

Anne made no contact with anyone at school; she would just sit apparently engrossed in her own preoccupations, regardless of everything that was happening around her and apparently oblivious of the efforts being made by the teacher and the other children to attract her attention. When the children moved from one room to another, Anne had to be picked up and carried, as the teacher said, 'like an inanimate doll'. The only exception to this was when anyone came near her wearing shining or sparkling jewellery. Anne would apparently notice this out of the corner of her eye (since she was never seen to look directly at anything or anyone) and if the person wearing it came near her, her hand would shoot out to grab at the jewellery as she attempted to wrench it off the person's neck or dress. Her grip was so strong and her fingers so tiny that it was extremely difficult to disengage them. If, however, the attempt to do so succeeded and she was unable to clutch at the object again, she would savagely bang her head on the floor, the door or the table. When the psychiatrist had completed his investigations he diagnosed that Anne was either severely subnormal or, more probably, suffering from that form of childhood psychosis known as infantile autism (for a detailed discussion of autism, see chapter 9). At about the same time the school informed him and the parents that they really could see no point in Anne's coming to them any longer. The school medical officer attempted to assess her intelligence and found that she was quite impossible to test. Her parents were therefore informed that Anne had been found to be unsuitable for education in school. As it happened, after treatment in a special educational unit, Anne started full-time attendance in a normal school in September 1968.

Anne was fortunate in that at the time that she was excluded from normal school her parents lived in one of the very few parts of the country where a special educational unit suitable for her needs existed. Although by law this should now be universally so, in fact progress in providing these units is painfully slow. One child, moving early in 1972 from an area where there was such provision to another part of the country, spent from January to September at home with only two extremely brief spells of attendance, first in a school for slow-learners, then in a junior training school. With all the goodwill in the world both establishments had to request his withdrawal as they were totally unable to meet his needs. By September the parents were desperate for some relief and have accepted a day placement in a group at a local subnormality hospital, until such time as either a vacancy in an existing school for autistic children occurs, or a new one is formed. The child has now experienced two rejections and has lost months of educational time. Only the strong family bond which fortunately existed, has prevented serious damage being done to the whole family. Unfortunately this type of case is far from unique. A report published (1972) by the National Society for Autistic Children *Their Right to Learn and Live*[2] claims that only 300 autistic children out of an estimated total of 6000 in Britain, i.e. 5 per cent, are receiving the specialist education which is now their statutory right. The claim is made that in consequence over 700 of these children have been incorrectly placed in subnormality hospitals. In fairness it should be stressed that some local authorities are in the process both of making and of planning extremely good provision, others, unfortunately are more tardy.

I shall return to certain features of Anne's story later, namely the diagnostic and educational aspects involved in such a situation. Her case seems to be one where normal development is arrested. In the next two examples, by way of contrast, the children initially seemed normal, but their conditions, due to undetermined factors, started to decline.

Pauline is the youngest child in a family of six and was born when both her parents were nearing forty. Both her parents and also her older brothers and sisters were completely normal and healthy and there is no history of mental illness in the family. Although the pregnancy was normal the birth was three weeks later than expected and the actual labour a long and difficult process culminating in a forceps delivery. All her early development was normal or early and she was an active, adventurous baby. When she was about two and a half years old and suffering from a heavy cold with some bronchial trouble, she began at times to tremble violently, then to rush into a corner of the room where she would remain still with her eyes fixed for about five seconds. A year and a half later she developed a high temperature and was obviously feeling very unwell. This persisted for some days at the end of which she had a long and severe fit of major epilepsy and during the next few days this was followed by several more fits. She was rushed to hospital where she was seen by two specialists who put her on drugs to control her epilepsy. Since her behaviour was disturbed she was also seen by a psychiatrist who afterwards saw her once a week for lengthy periods.

She went to the local infants school but, according to her parents, 'learned nothing'. At seven she was admitted again to hospital and after a period of treatment with a different drug was taken off drugs altogether for six months. During this time she seemed to be much better, could be 'talked to' and also learned to read. She then went to a special boarding school. Some months later she became ill, her fits recommenced and she was put back on drugs. She no longer appeared to be learning anything, became very disturbed and was ultimately excluded from her boarding school. She was readmitted to the hospital and it was found that her score on intelligence tests was much lower than it had been the year before. This period of Pauline's life proved to be typical of the next few years. Her ability to learn appeared to be steadily decreasing and her behaviour became progressively more disrupted and disturbed. She was excluded from another school and sent to a special school for slow-learners which also excluded her because of her disturbed behaviour. Ultimately she, like Anne, was officially declared to be unsuitable for education at school. After a further spell in hospital she was fortunately offered a vacancy in a Rudolph Steiner school where she still is.

Peter is a second child. As in the case of Pauline, all other members of his family are normal and healthy. His parents were delighted when he was born; their elder child was a girl and they had hoped the second would be a boy. Until he was three Peter developed normally in every way, including starting to talk. One day he fell down the stairs, but this did not seem to affect him badly, and there has never been any evidence to show that his fall affected his subsequent behaviour. His mother, however, still wonders. The first sign that things were going wrong was when his speech began to deteriorate. He suddenly seemed unable to bring out words which he had been using fluently. This steadily became more noticeable. Then, as his mother puts it, he 'began to try to shape the words with his mouth and would put his hands up to it and manipulate them as if he was desperately trying to force his mouth to make the sounds or as if he was trying to pull the words he wanted out with his hands'. His parents, who were seriously worried by now, took him from hospital to hospital trying to get advice and help. He was investigated for deafness and was also seen by many specialists. The mother was told that he was clearly subnormal and advised to 'put him away and forget him'. When he reached school age he was seen by a school medical officer and found to be unsuitable for education at school. He was sent to a training centre where he quickly outstripped the other children in his ability to do puzzles, etc. However, his speech was now completely gone, although he made loud grunting and other noises. He became very restless and would sometimes frantically beat his own head or bite his hand. Eventually he became too disturbed in his behaviour for the training centre staff to cope with him so his mother was asked to keep him at home. He was investigated at a special diagnostic centre for non-communicating children and once again the parents were told that he was not suitable for treatment at the centre. His mother was pregnant again and found the strain of looking after Peter day in and day out almost more than she could bear. With her husband she took him to see yet another specialist at another hospital. Although he could offer the parents little hope and also freely admitted that he was unable either to account for, or to diagnose, Peter's condition, he did offer to allow Peter to visit one of his units for subnormal children for a period of six months. The parents accepted the offer gratefully because it did, at least, give the mother some relief; in fact he stayed at this unit for twelve months. However, it was as before: gradually his achievement, except in speech, outstripped the other children's, he became difficult and frustrated and finally after he had been involved in a fight with two of the older children, he reverted to biting himself savagely – then one of the other children – and so once again he was excluded. This time his mother really felt she was alone and did not know where to turn next for help. She went to a meeting of the National Society for Mentally Handicapped Children and heard a speaker describe how she had, after similar experiences, decided to prove that her child could be educated by teaching him herself and how this had led eventually to his being accepted in a special boarding school. Peter's mother decided to try to do the same, in spite of the fact that she now had the new baby to look after in addition to all her other responsibilities. Teaching Peter proved to be a hard and heartbreaking task, particularly as he got very angry with her when she persisted and insisted that he should do the tasks she felt were within his capacity, and would not let him 'escape into his own world'. Finally, however, his achievement was so much greater that she obtained an interview for him to be considered for admission to one of the Rudolf Steiner schools. He was accepted and offered a place but since there was no way in which the parents could possibly afford to pay all the fees themselves they applied to the Local Education Authority for assistance.

Within days they were informed that since Peter had been found to be unsuitable for education in school there was no way in which the authority could help with the fees. All appeals only evoked the same response. Eventually when their doctor warned them that the mother's health was being severely affected by the strain, and when they noticed that their younger daughter was beginning to show signs of becoming frightened when Peter had one of his violent noisy fits of self-attacking, the parents sadly and reluctantly accepted the only provision that was offered to them – a bed in a ward for severely subnormal children.

Peter is now nearing adulthood. His placement was somewhat improved when his mother, desperate because of the marked deterioration that was taking place because of the totally unstimulating life he was subjected to on a subnormality ward, threatened to take him home and face the full, possibly tragic, consequences of this act if he was not moved. As a result a place was found for him in a psychiatric hospital where, at least, more sophisticated treatment was provided. However, it was not a ward for adolescents but for mentally-ill adult males. Peter's parents feel trapped in a hopeless dilemma, their present sorrow in no way alleviated by their dread of his future, particularly after they have died, or have grown too old to be physically capable of having him home periodically as they now do, to give him some personal care, comfort and love.

It is almost impossible to pinpoint the 'cause' of Pauline's and Peter's decline. For Pauline, damage at birth could be a possible factor, for Peter, his fall. Possibly there is some kind of organic damage, but even if this could be ascertained, it would provide no answer for future treatment. Nor would it be clear how this could be averted in other cases. In contrast, where environmental or social factors are decisive in causing a child to function below his potential, certain remedies seem obvious. It is no longer a matter of wondering what it is about a situation that causes a child to be subnormal. It is all too apparent. What one does wonder at instead is *why* the situation is allowed to continue. Can we not order our society better to remedy neglect, emotional insecurity, lack of a stable home, etc.?

The following story illustrates painfully clearly the seemingly inevitable downward path of a child whose normal family circle is inadequate.

Caroline's mother came from Ireland to find work and soon drifted into a relationship with a rather feckless Irish labourer who frequently lost his job for fighting when at work, particularly if he had been drinking. In consequence the mother became the chief bread-winner and continued to work after she discovered to her dismay that she was pregnant. She made a half-hearted attempt to abort the child but was quite glad when she didn't succeed. However, she made no attempt to get proper pre-natal care and became severely anaemic. Caroline was born in hospital after a long but normal labour. Both her parents were found to have active TB and were hospitalized for treatment. The baby was sent to official foster homes but soon had to be re-admitted to hospital where it was found that she had a congenital heart disease. Up to the age of eighteen months her life was divided between periods in hospital and in different foster homes. Her development was retarded in every direction. Both parents were successfully treated for their TB and when they were discharged from hospital, set up home together again. They had another child who appeared to be normally healthy and they maintained, as they still do, a spasmodic contact with Caroline. With steady care her physical condition improved and she learned to walk and to play but was very slow in developing any speech. She was admitted to a hospital for subnormal children and from then on for a time lived in one ward or other of this hospital, going home occasionally for fairly long holidays. This relatively regular pattern to her life was only established when she was over six years old and when she had had so many changes in her early childhood that she had formed no affectionate or stable relationships with anyone at all. Apart from her physical handicap she is a grossly deprived child. It is not surprising therefore that at seven she developed very severe temper tantrums which appeared to have started when she was prevented from taking from another child a toy which she clearly longed for. At this time she was attending the hospital training centre but was excluded because of her tantrums and 'spiteful behaviour' towards the other children.

Recently she has been transferred to another hospital of the same group and allowed to attend the hospital training centre. Is it any wonder that the teachers there reported that 'she was frightened and withdrawn and resented any attention at first'? Thanks to their patience and tolerance, and also to that of the staff on the ward where she now lives, Caroline is gradually becoming more friendly with the staff and is even beginning to speak, although she still has 'temper tantrums' when frustrated. She is learning quite quickly and is obviously benefiting greatly from the help she is getting at present – not least from the medical registrar who is in charge of her case. But what will her future be? The registrar will inevitably move on and the nursing staff will change. If she continues to improve, what are her chances of getting out of the hospital? Will she ever be considered, as she never has been yet, for education in an ordinary special school? How are her chances of improvement being affected by the life which she has led to far and is continuing to live at present?

Jim may indicate some of the possible answers for he is now twenty-eight and a patient in the same hospital. He does not stay on the ward all day as many of the patients do because he is a competent and useful worker. He has a fair vocabulary, can cope with money and is perfectly able to travel outside the hospital on public transport. He can also cope with his personal care and hygiene. Why, therefore, is he living in a hospital for subnormality? The chief answer seems to be that he is a member of a large family in poor circumstances and that his mother died when he was six. His father, a rather inadequate man overwhelmed with financial and other problems, had no relatives living near to help with the children when his wife died. The older children managed but Jim and his brother of seven didn't. As he says, 'we were naughty – always in trouble – and didn't go to school'. As they got older they got more difficult and finally into real trouble which involved the police. Their intelligence was assessed as low and their academic achievement as nil and so they were sent to hospital as they 'needed care and protection'. This was some years ago, of course, so they were admitted before all the recent improvements which have taken place in the education provided in the hospital 'schools'. This makes Jim's present achievements even more remarkable and compels one to wonder what he would have achieved had any other provision been available to him and his brother when they so badly needed it. The beginning of his story does not only belong to the past either, for it is probably true to say that all over the country at the present time there are children being admitted to mental and subnormality institutions for very much the same sorts of reasons.

Jonathon, Anne, Pauline, Peter, Caroline and Jim represent some of the many children who are subnormal. They all have different disorders, different backgrounds, different needs. What facilities are available to their parents to help them cope with their own child's particular handicap? From the preceding accounts it is evident that prompt diagnosis is difficult. In Anne's case, for example, there was for a time the suspicion that deafness was at the root of her trouble. The diagnosis of autism was not made until she was four years old, although she had been examined earlier in her life by a doctor and by a health visitor. Thus no remedial treatment was prescribed early enough to prevent her being found unsuitable for education in school.

A more callous example is found in the specialists' attitude to Peter's disabilities. Not only was there total lack of understanding of the parents' dilemma, but also a faiure to appreciate the results of his mother's efforts to train him. Once neatly categorized, he remained for ever 'unsuitable for education in school'.

The repercussions on the family of the birth of a handicapped child are many and extreme. Nothing can prevent the emotional, social and financial consequences, but much can be done to mitigate them. In this country we have the National Health Service, welfare and other services, which do, in fact, offer a great deal of assistance. Nevertheless, perhaps not enough is done to assuage the stress that parents of a handicapped child are subjected to. Several writers have already commented to this effect.

Although services have been greatly extended and improved since the Mental Health Act of 1959, we believe more could be done to ease the burden of families caring for a mentally handicapped child or adult. . . .

In post-war Britain it comes as a shock to parents to find themselves in a situation that is not fully covered by the welfare state. As long as the society in which we live accepts the child in principle but not sufficiently in fact, the problems of acceptance are made harder than they need be for the parents and the child. It is not easy to accept a situation unless society also accepts it.[3]

Acceptance by society is not easy to achieve, however. As Peter Mittler states, 'Plans to integrate the care and treatment of the mentally subnormal with general medical, psychiatric and community services will have to overcome initial deep-rooted prejudices.'[4] These 'prejudices' are both communal and individual – anyone who has attempted to find premises in which to set up any sort of provision for the mentally handicapped knows only too well the kind of difficulties involved. Planning permission must be obtained and opposition is usually raised by the local residents who give as their reason that having such provision in their midst will 'reduce the value of their property' – a good reason if true, but totally unsupported by available evidence. When sites for a training centre were proposed to the Planning Officer of one of the largest seaside towns on the south coast it was the *sixth* suggestion which was accepted. The town was more fortunate than most in having this number of possible sites. The one for which permission was obtained was on the very limit of the town and hidden from the road by trees. It is very beautiful, but its location not only increases the distances which the children have to travel daily to reach it, but also creates great difficulties for the staff who are trying to educate children to live in the community which could only find room for them on its fringe. This is typical of the problems faced on the administrative level, and they are frequently made more galling by the apparent praise which cloaks the refusal: 'You are doing wonderful work – but please do it away from me.'

This is the community attitude even where excellent facilities are provided by the community; the parents constantly face manifestations of it from the time their child is born. Many experience it first by the way in which they are told or are left to find out that their baby is not normal. A survey carried out in London in 1954 concluded that 'in very many instances the communication of the discovery of mental defect was handled very badly'.[2] The same survey revealed that only 31 per cent of the parents interviewed were given positive confirmation that their child was subnormal before the baby was one year old, 32 per cent before five years old and 37 per cent after the child had reached school age. Fifty-eight per cent had actually been told of their child's condition; the rest claimed that they were left to find out for themselves. When asked when they would recommend that parents should be told, 89 per cent felt that the doctor should discuss the matter with the parents as soon as he suspected the child's condition.

There were great differences in the way in which the news had been broken. In 14 per cent of the cases the situation was poorly handled. Some babies were demonstrated to students as idiots in the mothers' presence, although the mothers themselves had been told nothing of the condition. In 41 per cent of the cases there were unsatisfactory features: vague statements that the baby was 'backward' but would improve. Of those who felt that the way in which they had been told was satisfactory, very few were fortunate enough to be given either the time or the opportunity to assimilate the news, or to see the doctors concerned frequently enough to discuss the diagnosis and its consequences, or to be given helpful and constructive advice over a period of time.

An extremely small number of the parents concerned had been given specialist advice as to the desirability of having more children and strangely, although it worried them greatly, only 33 per cent had sought and obtained any form of advice about this matter. Unfortunately, many who did so had been ill-informed by their GPs. At a recent conference in Leeds organized by the National Society for the Mentally Handicapped, Kenneth Selly, when discussing this point, indicated the need for the right sort of training for GPs to be provided in medical schools regarding subnormality. He quoted the case of a GP acquaintance who had owned to having covered the whole subject of mental health during his training by spending three afternoons in a mental hospital. Unfortunately, by all accounts this is not uncommon.

The following extracts are from the story of one handicapped child, 'Molly', which was told by her mother at an Annual General Regional Meeting of the National Society for Mentally Handicapped Children. They exemplify the experiences of some mothers of handicapped children.

This is the beginning of the story, a beginning which at first seemed to my husband and I to be the end, even though realizing the difficulty of diagnosing anything unusual in a very young baby, I feel that the matter was not treated with the sense of urgency that my husband and I had known instinctively was required!

After some months of investigations, Molly's mother, when Molly was eighteen months old, asked the paediatrician outright what was really wrong with her.

I had thought that his previous answers to my hesitant questions had been made merely to 'put me off'. It was then that he told me that apart from the visible effects which we all knew, he could not honestly say what had happened to cause Molly's illness. Strangely enough, the confession that he did not know was to me far more comforting than would have been an attempt to raise false hopes.

As the years passed for Molly her parents never ceased to seek help and advice but on every hand they failed to find it – she was admitted to a training centre but quickly excluded from it on the grounds that 'she was a positive nuisance to the class'. A new paediatrician saw her at the hospital who 'did not seem very sympathetic'; for example, when asked for advice about her right foot which was beginning to turn in, the reply was, 'Well, she can walk on it–put her two left shoes on.' Later when permission was sought for another interested doctor to meet her, Molly's mother was told that 'nothing can be done for her; she should be taken home and put to bed both for her own good and for the good of the community.' 'And so for the second time in a few months Molly was again rejected and this time I felt really alone.' During the years that followed

when one would have expected to use the local authority services, we coped entirely without their help although the welfare visitors from the Mental Health Department have come and gone throughout the years and having approved of the way we have managed, have continued to let us do so. I have never made an issue of this but in the early days and indeed throughout the years, one of my main needs has been expert advice. I would have expected that this would have been within the scope of the local authorities, but whenever I have sought it, I have been told, 'Oh, you're doing fine and if you continue like this you don't need us to tell you what to do.'

I have needed advice about the mundane things such as teeth and eyes and, more serious, about the increasing deformity of Molly's right foot. I have usually been told to seek it through the normal channels. But what does one do when a child screams the waiting room down and kicks the dentist and his nurse? It's no use having her eyes tested because she can't read, and anyway she would fight and break the spectacles if she had to wear them. What does one do when the doctor again contacts the paediatrician and he again repeats that nothing can be done about her foot owing to her mental state? What does one do when, through continuous pestering, the paediatrician promises eventually to find another specialist (at one's own cost) and one is still waiting after ten years?

How often I have wished that a few of these simple burdens could be taken from my shoulders and how often have I wondered whether it is just because my child is at home and not at a training centre that the Mental Health Department, who are supposed, surely, to have some duty to her, cannot be bothered to help, except for the welfare visitor referring to 'usual channels'. Perhaps if I had been more incompetent I would have received some help.

Comment would add nothing to these true experiences of a typical case of a mother of a handicapped child who felt that she had failed to find help. If this case were unique it would be bad enough. Unfortunately, there is a great deal of evidence in the case histories that it is far from being so.

Molly's story started some years ago. Ralph is still only seven. There is no doubt that he is a severely subnormal child, for he is slightly microcephalic, which means that his head is abnormally small. He has some ability, though, and can learn – this he proves by his actions; for example, he is quite able to plug in, switch on and select his favourite television programmes. His parents accept his subnormality and also that his behaviour can be disturbed, but they wish to keep him living at home with them for as long as they can manage him and they also want him to have some form of education or training. Both of these wishes seem reasonable and also justifiable on human and economic grounds. It is no longer believed that if a child is ultimately going to need residential placement, the sooner he gets it the better. In fact the reverse has been shown to be true – the longer a child can be contained within the loving care of his own family, the higher his level of functioning can become and also the greater his emotional stability and maturity, so that the later he has to go to an institution the better he can sustain it. One would have thought therefore that Ralph's parents would have been given encouragement and support. He was admitted to a day training centre but excluded after a few weeks. The parents became very uneasy and took him to a specialist who said, 'Ralph has some autistic tendencies' – without telling them the simple truth about the child. After a while when the whole family was feeling the strain of trying to cope with every aspect of Ralph's training and behaviour without help or support, the parents accepted the only relief they were offered, namely, a residential placement in a mental subnormality hospital. Ralph was disturbed on admission, so the parents were asked not to visit him for a period so he could get 'settled in'. They wished to cooperate and so complied with this request and he became quieter and 'easier to manage' in the hospital, but violently aggressive to his mother on every subsequent occasion when they were allowed to take him out or home for the weekend. This was heartbreaking for the parents since previously with all their sad experiences, they had had the comfort of having a loving child. They were also very worried that Ralph was not properly placed, for articles were appearing suggesting that autistic children could be helped to achieve with proper education, and the only diagnosis they had been given was the suggestion that he was 'mildly autistic'. Ultimately, and against the advice of the hospital which predicted correctly that the parents would have difficulty in getting him admitted to a training centre, they removed him. They were also warned that if they relinquished his hospital bed they might have difficulty in getting it back again. This is also a strictly realistic statement since there are always waiting lists for hospital beds. However, as the mother says,

we prayed very hard . . . and we felt very strongly to keep him home, so of course we discharged him ourselves. Now we are being told by the authorities we should not have done so. We can get no help anywhere. . . . The training school at Y has turned us down saying Ralph needs more attention than they can give with their large classes. Also, where he was before, for a few weeks' observation, has turned him down. In each case I offered to go with him to see he didn't run away.

This was the reason given for him being excluded from both

places previously. The next nearest training centre is some distance away,

and they won't provide transport for him, we are too far away. . . . All we can think of is to approach training centres in other towns and if one will accept him we shall have to move. . . . The authorities won't provide any help whatsoever, no cheap milk, no baby sitter, yet they were willing to pay pounds a week to keep him in hospital, plus lovely clothes for him. He is not as well-dressed now! Also, I have not had one word of advice as to how to help Ralph at home. Home teachers are available on paper but in actual fact they are non-existent.

In addition to all this, Ralph's mother was thoroughly alarmed because she was finally told he was severely subnormal, which he technically is, but since no one explained the term to her, she interpreted it as meaning that he was not fit for the training centres and asks, 'But who will have him when he has been classified as severely subnormal?'

I spoke at a meeting in a Midlands town and a mother and grandmother of a nine-year-old epileptic child stood up in the audience appealing for help and advice. They had just received an official letter baldly stating that the boy would be excluded from the boarding school for epileptics where he had been placed by the authorities as he had 'not proved to be suitable'.

These three true stories are typical. In each case there are things to be said in favour of the authorities, in Molly's case, the different welfare workers concerned were probably each responsible for a very heavy case load and so, seeing that Molly was being well cared for, simply did not spare the time to inquire further, nor to appreciate how desperately the mother needed their sympathetic understanding. In Ralph's case, the hospital authorities, knowing the local problems and having had experience of his personal difficulties, wanted the parents to accept what they had decided was the right solution. The school the epileptic boy was attending had obviously proved to be the wrong choice.

The sad common factor in these cases is the break-down in communication between the parents of the children and the authorities. In none of them does there appear to have been the faintest appreciation of the feelings experienced by these parents who clearly all felt that they and their children were being rejected and left without help from any source.

There are, unfortunately, many other similar cases. In the Annual Report of the Ministry of Health for the year 1966, the total number of subnormal and severely subnormal persons of all ages receiving Mental Health services was given as 93,486. Of these, 36,819 are receiving training either at home or in day training centres while 4254 are receiving residential care from the local health authorities. The remainder (about 52,000) are in hospitals. One of the most important decisions which the parents of any mentally handicapped child must make is whether to keep the child at home in the family or to seek residential provision for him. This is a question which they alone should decide, although help should be easily available for them while they are making their choice. The figures quoted above, while not totally comprehensive, indicate how many parents are keeping their handicapped children at home.

The survey previously quoted[2] demonstrates that the families who did this were in every respect less well off in consequence. They were significantly more over-crowded in the home and in addition 33 per cent had some other housing problem. Many more of them were rated as being financially 'poor' and this was directly due to the fact that they had to support an extra dependent member. This fact at least has now been modified for some of the families concerned. As recently as 1970 no help of any kind was offered by the community to those parents, who, by keeping their handicapped member at home, were effectively saving the nation at large vast sums which would otherwise be required to make residential provision for them all. Now some 80,000 people who are so disabled that they require constant care both day and night, receive an Attendance Allowance (at present £4.80 per week) designed to help to provide this care. It has been estimated that by 1975 the number receiving some kind of allowance will have increased to 300,000 at a total cost of £70,000,000. Great though this help and relief undoubtedly is, it is still subject to much critical comment. There is some evidence of inconsistencies in its administration, complaints that parents are not being given sufficient help and guidance by their General Practitioners when filling in the forms together with a growing feeling of jealousy and bitterness and misunderstanding between the parents whose claims have been accepted and those who have been rejected. The comment is even frequently made that local social workers appear to be unaware of the total provisions possible under the scheme. In time to come the outcome may be that the whole scope of the provision is so widened that every disabled person will receive some allowance, varied only by the degree of their handicap. Nevertheless none of the criticisms should be allowed to obscure the great relief and advantages the provision of the Attendance Allowance and the speed with which it was put into effect have brought to many of the affected families.

To return to the findings of the survey the other problems still remain. The social contacts of these families were seriously limited, the difference between the two groups being highly significant and clear evidence of the restricting effect that a handicapped child in the family has on the social intercourse of the parents. Nevertheless, although this kind of evidence demonstrates that 'community care', as advocated by the Mental Health Act of 1959, is only too often provided at the expense of the family group, very few of these families were considering residential placement and 29 per cent of those who in fact had had to seek it mentioned that 'they might have been able to keep their child at home had adequate medical or social services been available at the time'. The reasons for placement were as follows:

In 5 per cent of the cases the child presented a problem of management.

In 20 per cent there was a family problem.

In 6 per cent medical advice or social circumstances were the determining factor.

In 11 per cent the mother's health was the deciding factor.

Kushlick found that:

The need for residential care arises either when the severely subnormal child makes excessive demands on an intact family or when the family, handicapped by sickness, death or the birth of another child, is unable any longer to cope with him.

It is apparent therefore that there will always be a certain number of children for whom residential placement is necessary and desirable, even though this number might well be reduced by the provision of more help for the families wishing to keep their children at home for as long as possible.

It will be interesting to assess after a period when the effect of the Attendance Allowance has had time to show whether this is in fact proving to be the case.

Part Two
The Severely Subnormal

Chapter Three
Residential Provisions

By far the greatest amount of residential care for the severely subnormal is provided in hospitals. This has traditionally been the case, and it would be foolish to pretend that it will not be so for some years to come. Nevertheless in the last few years there has been growing public awareness of all that this implies and an increase of dissatisfaction with the way of life this kind of provision offers to its inmates. Several unfortunate scandals and evidence of malpractice in a few cases have highlighted this concern. While not in any way condoning these events, it has seemed to me at times that too little public attention has been drawn to the incredibly difficult conditions imposed mainly by shortages that the staff of these hospitals work under, shortages not only of personnel but also of money. Taken in conjunction with the age and inconveniences of many of the actual hospital buildings the attempts that have been made to improve the standards of condition and care merit great praise. This, however, does not change the fact that what is needed is a radical alteration of the whole of the provision. Such an alteration is now official policy for in 1971 the Department of Health and Social Security issued a White Paper *Better Services for the Mentally Handicapped* Command 4683 which sets out future planning in this respect. This White Paper is comprehensive and complex and certain aspects of it will be discussed later in this chapter. Overall it is aimed at providing for the mentally handicapped and their families a triple choice of excellent facilities. (1) Well-supported home care, (2) civilized hospital care and (3) well-supported community care. This is the ideal aimed at, but it is realistically stated that it will take up to twenty years to achieve even if all financial and other problems are resolved. In view of this it is necessary to describe the present position and the attempts which are now being made to modify it, since this is, in fact, what the children and their parents can expect to find, before going on to consider the implications of the White Paper.

The subnormality hospitals are usually comprehensive institutions situated either in the country or on the outskirts of a town. They frequently contain a thousand or more beds for adult and child patients of all grades of subnormality. Thus they have to provide care for a wide variety of cases and are sometimes the only places willing to accept and help some of the most difficult patients.

The facilities offered by these hospitals are dependent for money on the National Health Service and their allocation is less per patient per week than for other types of hospitals. Until the transfer of educational responsibility to the Department of Education and Science (which became effective in 1971) the hospitals provided from their own resources such educational provision as they felt necessary and financially possible.

This chapter will examine the basis on which children are admitted to these hospitals, the pattern of hospital life and ways to modify it and the fundamental alteration to the educational provision which is now taking place in consequence of the transfer of responsibility.

Admission

The Mental Health Act of 1959 redefines the categories of mental handicap in the following way. The term 'severely subnormal' replaces the earlier definitions of 'idiot' and 'imbecile'. Into this category fall those cases in which there is,

a state of arrested or incomplete development which includes subnormality of intelligence and is of such a nature or degree that the patient is incapable of living an independent life or of guarding himself against serious exploitation, or will be so incapable when of age to do so.

A second category of 'subnormal' is defined as,

a state of arrested development of mind (not amounting to severe subnormality) which includes subnormality of intelligence and is of such a nature or degree which requires, or is susceptible to, medical treatment or other special care or training of the patient.

The IQ plays some part in assigning people to these categories. The intelligence quotient is a statistical concept which gives a level of function. (The method of calculating an IQ is described in chapter 5, pp. 107–8. On a standardized intelligence test the average score is 100, and 95 per cent of the population will fall within the range from 70 to 130. The classification of severely subnormal is generally used for those whose IQ is 50 and below but assessment should never be dependent merely on IQ scores; social factors must also be taken into account. At this low level of function it is frequently impossible to obtain a measure of any kind, and so this category also includes children who, because they function below the level of the test or because their cooperation cannot be obtained, have been assessed by other means. Into the category of subnormal fall those who score between 50 and 79. The normal range of intelligence is considered to start at 80.

One would expect, therefore, to find in a subnormality hospital only those children who fail to achieve a score of 50–55 or above, i.e. the severely subnormal. This does not seem to be the case. In a survey conducted by the British Psychological Society, seventeen hospitals gave details of admissions of children during 1962. This covered about 30 per cent of the total admissions for that year in England and Wales. Nearly three-quarters of the children were classified as severely subnormal; just under one-sixth were in the subnormal range; the remainder were suffering from psychopathic disorders or mental illness. Some of the younger children were withdrawn or inaccessible and thus unclassified, and there were a small number for whom no information was available. Of the total number 23 per cent had additional, physical handicaps.[1]

A standard test was administered to 155 of these children. Ninety-eight (constituting 24 per cent of the total admissions covered in the sample) had IQs of over 50. Fifty-seven had scores above 70 and a further fifteen above 100. These figures are confirmed by other surveys. (In fact the numbers are higher for older patients.)

It seems justifiable, therefore, to conclude that many children are admitted to these hospitals not because they are severely subnormal but because there is no suitable alternative available to them. They do not need special treatment for physical handicaps or severe emotional disorders, although some of them present behaviour problems which interfere with their education in normal schools. In my own experience, disturbed children in care of local authorities are particularly at risk in this respect as they are unsuitable for fostering and are disruptive in a normal children's home. At present they are often neither suitably placed, nor, as we shall see later, properly educated.

The severely handicapped

Those most obviously in need of hospital care are the most severely affected children: those with crippling and multiple handicaps. At present these children are either at home (if their families can cope) or in psychiatric hospitals. For some of them most forms of education or training are precluded. They are probably the only ones who do need hospital care, and those not at present in hospitals will eventually need hospital treatment in the future.

Regarding the provision for these children the question is, should they be segregated as they are at present? J. Tizard, who has wide experience as a leading research worker in this area, makes an alternative suggestion.[2] He proposes that those children who require hospital services could sometimes be placed in ordinary children's wards, 'but most would live in long-stay annexes to children's wards or hospitals'. Thus, 'hospital services would be available for all children whose main need was for nursing and medical care, e.g. most idiots, gross hydrocephalics, the bedfast'.

The leading role in the treatment and care of such cases would be assumed by the paediatrician who, Tizard points out,

would so gain experience in dealing with a wide range of chronic physical diseases, many of which are still undiagnosable and a challenge to research. Their experience in other fields of child health and disease would enable them to see the problems of mental defect in a wider concept. Teaching, too, would be facilitated.

The over-all importance of seeing 'the problems of mental defect in a wider context' cannot be overemphasized, and is applicable to all aspects of the care of all severely subnormal children.

Tizard proposes that the day-to-day management of the special annexes should be in the care of nurses and medical auxiliaries some of whom, notably the sisters in charge, would remain permanently on the ward; they would be there because they were 'dedicated women' (one would add, or men) who had chosen to 'give their working lives to the nursing of idiots'. The other members of the staff would be temporary and working in this annexe to widen their experience and as an essential part of their training. The suggestion is made that a general children's hospital might gain rather than lose by the added responsibility placed upon it, and since placement in a general hospital would ensure the availability for all of the full hospital services such as laboratory and electrophysiology, new discoveries and solutions to diagnostic and clinical problems would be much more easily made. The benefit to the patients would be two-fold. 'A greater range of specialist services would be brought to bear upon their condition' and they would profit even more from the 'individual care able to be given in a small well-staffed unit.'

It is worth noting that a working party set up by the Paediatric Society of the South-East Metropolitan Region said of Tizard's plan that they were 'impressed by the possibilities of this idea',[3] and further commented:

Some of the younger children in this group are already in children's hospitals or in paediatric wards of general hospitals. We think there is a very strong case for increasing their number for two cogent reasons. The first of these is the very fact that paediatric wards are not fully occupied and that the need for paediatric beds will continue to decrease; the second is that the work of the paediatricians themselves has altered in a quite emphatic way and in a direction which is likely to continue away from the diagnosis and treatment of acute illnesses and towards the study and care of children with continuing disorders, such as epilepsy, cerebral palsy and mental disorder to a degree which in some centres makes the paediatrician well fitted to act in the assessment of a subnormal child (pp. 14–15).

There is of course a further function of the paediatrician – his responsibility for the new-born in maternity hospitals where from 70 to 80 per cent of children in England are born. Here the paediatrician is in the best position to diagnose the earliest signs of developmental disorder, and to study their causes.

Kushlick makes a complementary suggestion.[4] He would set up small 'family homes' situated in areas of 100,000 population, so that all the children in residential care would be living in the same area as their parents which would facilitate visiting, etc. This suggestion will be further discussed later in this chapter. The plan would include in each family of ten children an average of three incontinent, bedfast children since this is the probable incidence of cases. These children would be cared for by a permanent staff which would include nurses, and would receive routine medical care from general practitioners who would make use, as required, of the specialist services provided by the local authorities and hospital services. An accurate assessment of the cost of this provision indicates that it might well be very little different from the vast sums that would be required to adapt and improve the existing institutions. Both of these plans are constructive and possible and offer a far better way of life to very handicapped children.

The severely subnormal and the subnormal

Having suggested alternative provision for the severely handicapped child, there still remains the great majority of children at present resident in mental hospitals. These include the mobile, if not always ambulant or continent, severely subnormal children, many of whom are multiply handicapped, the subnormal children and the children who, as the BPS survey* showed, should not be in mental hospitals at all, but are admitted largely because of either behaviour problems, or more frequently, because of a total lack of other more suitable provision being available. The question to be asked is 'why are all these children in hospitals?' The answer is simple: they are in them, not because they are ill nor because their prime need is medical care and skilful nursing, but purely because the hospitals are there. The reason for this state of affairs is historical. Initially it was believed that the subnormal child or adult could not be improved, that he could

* Although the BPS survey referred to was published in 1966 and carried out in 1962 its findings are still valid, for in this respect there has been no significant change.

not learn or acquire any skills, even (except in rare instances) how to cope with his own personal hygiene and care. He would therefore always need to be safeguarded and cared for in a closed community. As already discussed, many of these children are multiply handicapped and since they are untaught, very few of them achieve simple skills or even continence, thus a hospital seemed to offer the best form of custodial care. Recent research and experience appear to show that the fundamental hypothesis behind this form of provision is incorrect.

Aims to be achieved

H. C. Gunzburg, Director of Psychological Services in hospitals for the subnormal in the Birmingham area has clearly set out the desired concepts to be used for educating and developing severely subnormal children. He does, however, state: 'yet it must be appreciated that these words are used in their widest sense and that "education" and "teaching" do not carry the "academic" meaning usually associated with these words'.[5] This sentence is also true of all special education and, in fact, increasingly so in all normal schools!

The aim of training and education in the junior training centre can therefore be defined as helping the mentally handicapped to develop those skills and to obtain that knowledge which will enable him to live as happily and as socially competent as a child and later as an adult. In practical terms this will mean teaching the mentally handicapped those habits and skills which will make him socially acceptable, assisting him in learning how to live with others and how to make himself useful and developing as much as possible his ability to use and understand spoken language.

He goes on to discuss the children's emotional needs for love, warmth, a feeling of security and of achievement, all of which cannot be separated from their programme of 'education or training'.

It is interesting to compare these aims with those set out in a typical and very thorough American study. The Division of Special Education in Massachusetts published a curriculum guide for special class teachers.[6] The desirable goals to be aimed at are stated to be (p. 110 *et seq.*):

1. Physical health.
2. Mental health, under which are included emotional stability, personal adequacy and social competency.
3. Sensory training.
4. Motor skills.

Each of these goals is then broken down into specific aims. There would not be space enough to discuss them all in this chapter but it is worth noting that the need to encourage pride in good grooming, the use of appropriate clothing in different conditions, the regular practice of speech related to everyday experiences, and the provision of constant and recurring opportunities for experiences in the community as well as in the centre are stressed in all the specific aims and suggested activities. The importance of providing opportunities for achievement and of creating an atmosphere of acceptance, affection and approval in which the child can be helped to develop social competency is also emphasized.

It can be seen that there is close agreement between Gunzburg and the Massachusetts study on the aims of training and education for subnormals. So far there has been little attempt to establish how these aims are being fulfilled in the residential institutions, although it is a very common experience on visiting such an institution to feel that, on the whole, they are far from being achieved or even recognized. Professor Tizard, in a paper presented at the 1966 International Conference of the Association for Special Education, describes the findings of a research project which investigated the care and treatment of subnormal children in residential institutions.[7]

He makes the initial point that for the severely retarded residential provision is still essential (pp. 164–76). (It is clear from an earlier study by Tizard that the number of people requiring such provision increases with age: 35 per cent of those up to ten years of age compared with 99 per cent of those between sixty and seventy needed residential care.[2])

Tizard and his colleagues studied over a period of three years the care provided for children in six institutions. These comprised a mental subnormality hospital, a paediatric hospital for children with physical handicaps, two homes for normal children and two homes for subnormal children. The hospitals were run on traditional lines and were staffed by nurses. They were comparable with the homes for normal children in that they were all large institutions each catering for a similar age range. In all four there were more boys than girls and the majority of the children had been in residence for some years. Each institution was divided into wards or cottages and these also were similar to each other in that they all contained children of both sexes and of widely differing ages. They were, of course, dissimilar with regard to the children's handicaps. The two homes for subnormal children were smaller, but the combined IQ range of children in them was comparable to the range in the subnormality hospital. Thus it is feasible to make a valid comparison between the hospitals on the one hand and the homes on the other, and, more specifically, between the subnormality hospital and the two homes for the subnormal.

All six institutions were assessed on a specially designed eighteen-item scale of Child Management Practices in which the higher the score the more rigid the rules which are in force, the more block treatment there is of the inmates, the larger the social division there is between the children and the staff, and the fewer opportunities there are for individuality to be expressed. Both hospitals had high scores and there was no overlap between even the most liberal hospital ward and the most restrictive cottage in any of the children's homes. Tizard and his colleagues postulate,

that the reasons for the contrasting patterns of upbringing ... are to be found in characteristics of their social structure; the hospitals are hierarchical, over-departmentalized and too highly centralized. They are task orientated rather than child orientated. A narrow medical ideology leads staff to see themselves primarily in the role of treating patients.

These are the conclusions; they are significant and important enough to justify a closer examination so that we may assess how far the needs of the children were met in each institution. Their needs are presented as follows:

1. Training in self-help.
2. Development of ability to communicate mentally.
3. Development of social skills.

4. Provision of suitable materials and opportunities for meaningful occupation.

Their training, in fact, should be designed to change them from a liability to useful and appreciated helpers, and should take place in an environment of affection and warm acceptance.

The conditions in the institutions in Tizard's survey varied greatly: on the one hand there were the normal children of average intelligence in the two children's homes. The problems associated with their upbringing were mainly of an educational, physical or social nature. The children in the two hospitals, however, included many with multiple handicaps. In the paediatric hospital 70 per cent were non-ambulant, in the subnormality hospital 50 per cent. A large proportion of the children in both hospitals were incontinent, about half required help with feeding and very few could dress themselves without help. These inabilities can probably be assumed to result directly from the children's handicap in the paediatric cases, but this is unlikely to be true for the subnormal children. The children in the homes for the severely subnormal were much more competent although they too included the multiple handicapped.

As would be expected, the children in the normal children's homes had normal speech as had most of those in the paediatric wards; the remaining few could make themselves understood through speech. In the subnormality wards, however, 76 per cent of the children had no speech at all for practical purposes and 11 per cent merely used single words, from which it follows that only 13 per cent could use speech even in its simplest form. This again compared very unfavourably with the severely subnormal children in the homes. These gross additional handicaps cannot therefore be regarded as the necessary outcome of the children's subnormality, but possibly as the result of the hospital's fundamental failure to supply the children's basic needs.

Tizard and his colleagues compared the daily life of the children in the different milieux. In the homes the children lived lives which corresponded as closely as possible to those of children living at home with their parents. Bathing was done individually; the children used the toilet when they needed to and only the known bed wetters were lifted and potted at night by staff who knew them and their individual needs. At weekends staff and children alike had their lie-in and their time of getting up and going to bed was geared to the time needed by each child. Their food was ordered from a shop and cooked and prepared by house mothers who then ate with the children. They had their own pocket money to spend, their clothing was bought for them, and as soon as they were old enough they had a clothing allowance of their own. Their lives were free and unregimented. In the children's homes for the severely subnormal, one of which was run by a local authority and one by a voluntary society, the pattern of management was essentially the same, and in all these homes the children had the care and attention of individual house mothers.

The pattern is totally different in the hospitals. In most wards the night staff had the responsibility of getting the children toileted, dressed and ready for breakfast by 7.30 a.m. when the day staff took over. This meant that twenty handicapped children had to be dealt with – frequently children whom the night nurse did not know since, as Tizard reports, in a typical ward forty-two different night nurses were on duty in one year. The nurse had to wake each child in turn and either promptly sit him on a pot or take him to the toilet. After this they all had to be washed and either dressed and sat on their beds to wait, or left in bed in their night clothes. In two of the wards of the subnormality hospital this process started at 4 a.m., in nine at 5 a.m. and in the last five at 6 a.m. In the paediatric hospital three-quarters of the children were woken at 6 a.m., the rest at 7 a.m., but in the two paediatric wards which had subnormal children as patients, the children were for some curious reason woken up at 4 a.m.

After they were dressed all the children in both hospitals, with the exception of one ward in the subnormality hospital, stayed in the dormitories, some merely in or on their beds, some with toys and books. There was no change at all in this routine at the weekends; the only break or interruption in the whole ward routine throughout the week was for those children who left the wards to go to school. At night, bedtime ranged from 4 to 8 p.m. with 50 per cent going to bed at 5 p.m. Even the older, active school children went to bed between 6 and, for a very few, 8 p.m.

All meals were eaten in the day room and the staff never ate with the children. In consequence, while they were in hospital, no matter how long their stay, they never sat down to eat with an adult nor even saw an adult eat a meal.

Since there was such a high incidence of incontinence, toileting did present a problem. However, since the children were potted according to a schedule and not encouraged to go according to need, this might have had some effect upon the incidence. In both hospitals 50 per cent of the children had five communal sessions of toileting during the day, each taking approximately thirty minutes or more. Again, in 50 per cent of the wards all children had to stay in the lavatories until the last child had finished. In the evening this was followed by the bathing session and all the children had to remain in the bathroom in 50 per cent of the wards until the last child had been bathed and dried. This meant that they had all been in the bathroom from the time that toileting had started. A large proportion of their day was therefore spent in this way in the lavatories and bathrooms. In addition to this, in most of the wards the children were roused to be potted three times during the night and this was not uncommonly done to all the children in the ward and not just to those known to be incontinent.

Home for these hospitalized children is a bed in a dormitory with a large day room attached in which all their other activities, except school, take place. Their personal clothing and belongings are restricted in the main to coats, slippers, shoes, toothbrushes and combs; their hair is cut in uniform style by the hospital barber. They never see food in an uncooked state or other than delivered in a trolley from the central kitchen ready for eating. Toys are communal, sweets are rationed and there is restricted choice, if any. Their opportunities for spending money, visiting the local shops, travelling on public transport and paying their fare, and so on, are extremely limited although those who have parents who are able to visit and take them out are more fortunate in this respect. The person who puts them to bed is never the same as the one who wakes them up in the morning, and frequent staff movement and changes means that one or both of these is frequently a stranger. Clearly, such practices cannot possibly stimulate the child to develop to his full potential.

Several things must be borne in mind, however; in the first place Tizard's detailed research was done in one mental subnormality hospital only. There is no reason to doubt that it was carefully selected as a typical example but it is unlikely to represent either the best or the worst, nor is it ever reasonable to generalize from one example only. Nevertheless the same points could be made about the other institutions studied and the overall results are quite clear.

Tizard emphasizes that none of the obvious deficiencies of the hospital system should be interpreted as criticism of the staff as individuals or the hospitals at large. Basically, the main problem seems to stem from the fact that hospitals are run according to an ideology which gives priority to the medical diagnosis, the treatment of disabilities, the arrangement and carrying out of a duty rota, the adequate keeping of records, the need for the preservation of cleanliness and order in wards, and by people – namely doctors and nurses – whose professional training emphasizes the desirability of these aims; whereas the individual, social, emotional and human needs of the children demand a very different order of priorities.

It is, therefore, possible to argue that in all the cases and categories considered in this chapter, placement in a hospital is not going to fulfil the needs of these children, and to demand the immediate setting-up of alternative provision. Ostensibly the most desirable form would be hostels or homes similar to those now commonly run by the children's departments for children in the care of local authorities, and this kind of provision is in fact already beginning to be set up. Some very able and enlightened authorities also successfully find foster homes for some of the severely subnormal children in their care and pay the foster mothers on a reasonable scale for their services. In years to come it may be that the large mental subnormality hospitals will be totally replaced but it would be utterly unrealistic, even if it was agreed to be completely desirable, to pretend that this will be the case in the immediate future. The hospitals are there, and they are functioning with varied resources, facilities and success with trained staff whose combined knowledge and skill is of inestimable value.

The obvious immediate task, therefore, is to attempt to alter the existing practices so that the needs of the children are better provided for whilst at the same time experimenting and planning for the future in such a way that all new provision is aimed at modifying and replacing the existing provision in whatever is determined to be the best way, rather than extending and persisting in the traditional pattern.

Modifying the hospitals

Some useful pioneer work has already been done in both these fields. The best known experiment on the effects of modifying the pattern of care for an institutionalized subnormal child was the Brooklands experiment which was directed by Tizard and which lasted from the spring of 1958 to the summer of 1960. In this

an attempt was made to apply to imbecile children the principles of child care that are today regarded as meeting the needs of normal children deprived of normal home life . . . the residential nursery was chosen as a model upon which to run the new unit.[2]

The children for the new unit were boys and girls aged from four to ten and were selected from patients at the old Fountain Hospital. At the start of the experiment their average IQ was less than 25 points on the verbal scale of the Minnesota Pre-School Intelligence Test and nearly 40 points on the non-verbal scale (the norm is 100). Thirty-two children were selected and paired in two groups, matched for sex, age, intelligence and, to a certain degree, diagnosis; the thirty-two paired children were randomly allotted to either the control or experimental group. The experimental group was moved from the hospital to Brooklands, a detached, three-storeyed house set in ample grounds near Reigate. The building was late Victorian and not ideal for the purpose and the attractive site had its drawbacks. However, it formed a marked comparison to the cramped wards of the Fountain Hospital, which was set in very small grounds in a crowded suburb of outer London. The control group, of course, remained at the Fountain.

Half of the children were Mongols, one suffered from phenylketonuria and the rest were undiagnosed, but it was thought that their conditions involved severe brain injury. Initially the new unit faced many difficulties. In fact it was only in the second year that the organization was complete and in a sense the research was begun.

The children on transfer were severely retarded and none of the sixteen had useful speech. They were emotionally maladjusted, subject to intense and prolonged tantrums, aggressive and demanding. They were extraordinarily dependent upon adults and were unable to persist in or initiate any activities without adult support. Their attention span was very brief and they were extremely restless, they had no road sense, had little or no contact with each other and were quite unable to share. During the research period the children were gradually organized into two family groups with their own house mothers and their own sitting room which was also used for meals. The daily programme was based on a nursery-school pattern and designed to give much opportunity for diverse motor activities with play of various kinds and with various materials, music and movement, walks and visits. Toileting and washing breaks were taken at all the appropriate times of the day but were a family activity and occupied a relatively short space of time. Special attention was devoted to language training but by using all the opportunities that occurred naturally in the course of daily life.

At the end of the experiment the non-verbal IQ of the Brooklands children was not significantly different from those of the control group but there was a very marked difference in the development of their verbal mental age and the difference was getting progressively greater as time went on. In the two years the control group had only made six months measurable progress while the Brooklands group, on average, had improved by fourteen months. In addition to this they were far less emotionally maladjusted, their tantrums were much reduced, they could play co-operatively and form attachments to each other and to the staff. They were, moreover, affectionate, happy children who were busy, interested, confident and full of fun. Tizard concludes that 'in all these respects, the behaviour of the children at Brooklands was in striking contrast to their earlier behaviour in the parent hospital and to the behaviour of their peers who remained in hospital'. This experiment clearly suggests that this type of family care is much more beneficial to the children.

Some local authorities are now beginning to provide some hostels and children's homes, and it is indicated in the most recent revision of the Local Authority and Welfare Plans that, by 1974, 120 junior hostels catering for 2140 children will be available. If in fact this provision is made, it will mean that this service will have nearly trebled in ten years, since there were only thirty-seven such hostels in 1964. It is to be hoped that these hostels will be carefully planned and staffed and designed to be run on the Brooklands' lines – for it would be of no advantage at all to have them in preference to the larger hospital units unless they were so planned. In fact they might well be worse if they were remote, detached from the community at large and without access to social, educational and medical facilities. Nevertheless, even if the 1974 figure is achieved, the bulk of the residential provision for some time to come will be the responsibility of the Regional Hospital Boards, so it is in this direction that the improvements needed must be attempted.

There remains the present. Each year about 1300 children are admitted to subnormality hospitals in England and Wales where they will live the kind of ward life already described. Clearly ways of modifying and improving it must be sought. Between January 1964 and July 1967, an experiment was carried out by Stephen and Robertson, psychologists at Queen Mary's Hospital, Carshalton, which attempted to modify the environment in one ward and to evaluate and compare the progress made by the children in this experimental ward with those of their matched controls in other wards of the same hospital. Each ward in the hospital comprises a twenty-bed room and an adjacent day room. On the experimental ward the twenty children were divided into two matched family groups of ten and given one room each as their 'home' – this was used both for sleeping and day-time activities. The eleven children in the group with mental ages of eighteen months to two years and over, all attended, daily, a special nursery school class in the existing hospital school from which they returned 'home' for lunch. A special play programme was planned for those children with mental ages of less than eighteen months and this took place in the 'family' rooms during the period when the other children were at school. In addition, during the second year of the experiment it was possible to set up a carefully planned adventure playground for the use of all the children on a piece of land adjoining the ward. In this year also the local grammar school girls voluntarily came in to play with the children in the evenings and the researchers successfully found 'aunties' to visit some of the children who were not regularly visited by their parents.

Each week a discussion meeting was held and attended regularly by all members of the staff involved in the project and this proved to be extremely valuable as it not only kept the project under constant review but also helped to achieve a high degree of contact between the teacher, sister and charge nurse. This was not only useful and satisfying but also ensured that their work was really complementary. Although the full empirical results of this experiment have not been completely worked out as yet, certain conclusions can be drawn. It was shown that the relatively small group of very low-grade children, i.e. those with mental ages of under one year but with chronological ages of ten and over, did not respond to the training which they were given and made no better progress in feeding, dressing, toilet training, play activities, or response to people and to speech than did those in the control group. It appears, therefore, that these children present a special problem and one which will have to be considered particularly in relation to the staff directly involved in their care. The other children improved in many ways: they became more controlled in their behaviour and far less dependent on the constant protection and reassurance of security provided by the adults. They also began to be able to choose their own activities and to work and play constructively. With constant encouragement and stimulation of speech, the children became interested in books and learned not to damage nor destroy wall pictures at eye level. It was clear that although these children undoubtedly learn by using the same techniques and materials as are used for normal children of an equivalent mental age, nevertheless there are some fundamental differences which must lead to some modification. Basically, these arise from the facts that, firstly, they are physically much bigger and stronger and therefore the equipment designed for smaller children often needs modification. Secondly, they do have brains which are damaged and therefore not functioning normally. This leads to their having additional handicaps which affect both their behaviour and their motor activity. This finding applies to all severely subnormal children, but the experiment clearly showed how greatly the children of this group were affected in behaviour and development by the routine existence and very limited experiences that life in a hospital provides. The aggressive, destructive behaviour shown at first in the classroom situation was not only very similar to that shown by normal deprived children but 'also seemed to arise from their eagerness to devour new material and experiences'. They had to learn that there was 'no need to fight to come first'; they could all have a turn. Although from the very beginning attempts were made to encourage speech, group activities and imaginative play, the children had experienced so little that it was difficult to know what to talk to them about, 'and with the imaginative play – again we felt that lack of experience resulted in little raw material for them to draw on'. The special facilities and skilled attentions of all the staff concerned made some improvements but it seems clear that a major factor in the progress made by the children was the enrichment of their lives and the increase in their fund of experiences. This was made possible in the last years of the experiment when, with voluntary help and help from other members of the staff, it became possible to arrange frequent outings to local shops, parks, tea shops and people's houses. At the same time the children's appearance was greatly improved by their being provided with individually chosen clothes and normal hair styles.

It proved possible also to modify the environment on the ward in some ways. The number of toys was increased and the children were given places to keep personal possessions. Some of the more able children were allowed to help in the kitchen, both in the preparation of hot drinks and of their 'tea', which again slightly extended their experiences and participation in the activities of the adult world. The two great insoluble problems on even this experimental ward proved to be the frequent staff changes, particularly among the junior nurses, with all its consequences for the children and the staff, and also the shortage of space, when all activities for all the children had to take place in one room, so that even visitors had either to take out the child they were visiting or to cope with the demands for attention of every other child in the group.

In conclusion, this experiment highlighted the effects on the children's whole development of the paucity of experience that hospital life normally provides. It also showed that progress and improvements could be made, while at the same time demonstrating the problems caused by hospital routines and ward design, problems which do not appear to be intrinsically insoluble. The application of the findings of this experiment would greatly improve the lives of the children in hospitals and could be effected since most of the improvements suggested do not depend upon heavy financial outlay.

The Wessex experiment

In 1966–7 permission was given to the Wessex Regional Hospital Board to set up two 'experimental' children's hostels, permission which was later extended so that in all six children's and four adult hostels will eventually be established. Briefly the need for new provision had arisen because beds were becoming no longer available for residents of the region. Sufficient capital was therefore set aside for 450 additional beds. A working party was then set up to consider the various ways in which these beds could be provided. The main possibilities were to expand the existing hospitals, to build either one large or two smaller new hospitals, or to build small hostel units throughout the region to meet local needs. The working party visited institutions and units which were chosen to give examples of the highest standards of hospital or hostel care, and, ultimately concluded that hostel-type accommodation in small units would be the best. The four decisive factors which led them to this conclusion were as follows:

1. A 'local' service would be provided. This would not only enable the local authorities to play an active part but would also utilize and benefit from the experience they possessed.

2. A hostel-building programme would be flexible and could be varied to suit changing needs or local circumstances.

3. Continuity of care could be maintained between patients, their

families, GPs, hospital specialists, hostel and training-centre staff and social workers.

4. Capital costs of hostels are considerably less than hospitals and the running costs do not appear to be significantly greater.

One of the significant factors that led to this decision was the recognition by the working party of the need for developing 'public awareness that subnormal patients should not be cut off from the community in large hospitals and that the public has a part to play in the care of these patients'. It was also recommended that initially, at least, these hostels should be added to the existing hospital groups.

The first object of the experiment was to demonstrate that in fact such units were even practically possible. It had been predicted that eight major obstacles would prevent their success.

They were as follows:

1. It would be impossible to find suitable sites, because of local neighbourhood opposition.

2. It would be impossible to find and retain staff.

3. The admission of children would have to be selective, i.e. only CAN children* or those not needing 'skilled medical and nursing care' (as in the Brooklands experiment conducted by J. Tizard) would be admitted. The severely physically handicapped, 'non-responsive' children and those presenting severe behaviour disorders would not be containable in the new units, and would have to be excluded and returned to the existing hospitals. If not excluded, the severely behaviour-disordered children would harm the frail and upset the entire programme.

4. Most children in hospital are helpless, non-responsive idiots who would be incapable of appreciating their environment or inherently destructive of the fabric of the building.

5. If the admissions were non-selective, it would become impossible to avoid in the new units, anti-therapeutic qualities of care found by Raynes and King in existing institutions, e.g. 'Block Treatment – i.e. residents do everything simultaneously and in large groups, e.g. getting up, dressing, toileting, eating, recreating etc.'

*These children are: continent; ambulant; need no special care.

'*Rigidity of Routine* – i.e. the above routines are exactly the same irrespective of the day of the week or the month or season of the year.'

'*Depersonalization* – i.e. the residents do not have personal clothing, toys or effects.'

'*Social Distance* – i.e. staff wear uniforms, eat and live away from the residents and seldom communicate with the residents other than to give orders or to intervene in crises. The staff move from one unit to another at frequent intervals.'

6. The running costs would be prohibitive.

7. The administrative problems would be considerable.

8. The original statistics would not be valid in practice, i.e. the characteristics of the real children would be very different from those suggested by the statistics.

In fact all such problems either did not arise or were surmounted without major difficulty. Sites have been found for all the hostels as a result of collaboration between the hospital boards and the relevant local authority officers. In some cases there was minor opposition but this was overcome. Sadly enough in one instance the permission to allow a site to be used was withdrawn by the council after it had heard a deputation, this in spite of the fact that neighbourhood opinion was overwhelmingly in favour of the unit. No major difficulty has been found in recruiting staff. Only one child has had to be excluded from the hostels and this for purely medico-legal reasons. No child was found who could properly be described as a non-responsive vegetable, this although *all* children who qualified for residential reasons have been admitted to the hostels, the staff are constant and in sufficient supply (i.e. five to one) to ensure that the children always get individual and never 'block-treatment'. The running costs as at present calculated compare very favourably with those of keeping the children in hospitals, about £29 per week as opposed to about £28. No major administrative problems have arisen and the actual incidence corresponds pretty well with the estimated characteristics of the children, where it differs it tends to be in the direction of increased difficulty, i.e. the children are slightly younger, the proportion of non-ambulant children is higher and the proportion of continent, ambulant children with no serious behaviour difficulties slightly lower than expected. It is worth emphasizing that these hostels are successfully caring for a true cross-section of all the children and include some of the most difficult and most severely retarded.

The hostels have now been in existence for sufficient time for some preliminary observations to be made. On the practical side very little damage has occurred to the furnishings and equipment, this applies even to the carpets in spite of the number of incontinent children! Socially, improvements have arisen from the natural situation of children actually living with caring adults, rather than being 'looked after' by them. This is exemplified at mealtimes when children who could not feed themselves now can, and children who previously had to be under restraint for restless disruptive behaviour can now be left free. This is directly due to the fact that the staff are eating with them and at the same tables. No problems have arisen when children have become seriously ill, they have been attended by the GP and if necessary admitted to the local paediatric hospital. Orthopaedic care has also presented no difficulty.

Those children who will benefit go to the local junior training school. Their clothes are individual and to a certain degree purchased by the staff living in the hostel and not in bulk by the hospital authorities. Perhaps most importantly of all, the parents of the children are actively welcomed in the hostel and encouraged to play as full a role as they are able. They supply much of their own children's clothing, toys etc. and are not discouraged from doing so, as happens only too often in the hospital situation, partly, it is only fair to add, because of the practical difficulties of laundering etc. this would involve. The parents and the hostel staff therefore know each other and such knowledge properly handled can only be advantageous to all, not least the child.

Since the two new hostels have only been operational from January 1970 and December 1970 it is too soon for any other than preliminary deductions to be made. It does seem reasonable however to state that first, they have proved that such provision is feasible and economic and second, that the children are enjoying and responding to a much richer and more stimulating way of life than that provided in the hospitals.

Further implications of the Wessex experiment

The two hostels which are already established are providing for all the children in need of residential provision in two separate well-defined localities in the Wessex region. At present all the other children in the area remain in the hospitals. This fact has provided the research with an invaluable control group, both residential groups are also being compared with the children who live at home.

The information now being gathered in this way is still in the preliminary stage and in the process of being analysed. Certain interesting factors are already emerging. In general there seems little room for doubt that the 'hostel' way of life is both feasible, economically practical and provides a far better way of life than can be achieved by even the best hospital ward. It is perhaps not altogether surprising that Kushlick and his colleagues have concluded that the attitudes of the personnel involved are extremely important and that a true and fair evaluation and comparison of the different methods can only be achieved if all concerned have agreed their common aims.[8] The Regional Hospital Board and the Management Committees for the Wessex region have adopted as official policy that the operational policies used in the hostels shall be applied to the subnormality hospitals. Nevertheless differences in quality of care still exist. Three main factors appear, at this present stage of the investigation to be of the greatest importance and interestingly they are not the ones usually quoted, i.e. shortage of trained nursing and specialist medical staff, 'overcrowding' and the severe handicaps and behaviour disorders of the children.

The key factor appears to be the ratio of staff to children, in the hostels this never exceeds five children to one adult at any time of day, this is particularly observed at the times when the children need most individual attention, i.e. getting up time, going to bed, bath and mealtimes. This ratio never exists in the hospitals and where traditional routines and hours of duty are observed it is frequently the case that the least number of staff are available at the times when the children most need individual care. This one fact alone can account for much that is undesirable both in the barrenness of the environment and the rigid routines which prevail.

A second important factor appears to be the centralizing of all decisions which tend to be made by personnel who have little if any personal contact either with the children or the units in which they live. This contrasts sharply with the hostels where nearly all decisions which affect management and care are made by the people who are actually living with the children in the hostel.

The third main important factor is that, whereas the families of the children in the hostels all live in the neighbourhood, those of the children in the hospital units do not come from a defined area, but are unduly scattered. This automatically severely lessens the amount of outside contact these children have. The situation appears to be the consequence of the custom of admitting a new patient to whichever unit had an available bed.

The Wessex policy should ensure that these factors will be favourably modified in the immediate future. Since in all areas hospitals are going to provide a large part of the residential care for some time to come it must be hoped that all regional boards will consider adopting similar policies to those proved to be sound in this region. Hospital routines and hours of duty can be modified, the ratio of staff to children can be increased since the Wessex experiment has clearly demonstrated that there is no need for the staff to possess nursing or medical qualifications provided such specialized care is locally available when needed. The easing of the routines to allow of much more active parent co-operation might well help in this respect also.

There appears to be absolutely no logical or practical reasons why many decisions should not be delegated to the actual staff working with the children. Lastly, since all the people concerned already occupy a bed it would seem perfectly feasible to adjust matters over a period of time so that eventually all who come from one neighbourhood do live in local groups and as near as possible to their families.

White Paper - Command 4683 - Better Services for the Mentally Handicapped[9]

At this point and before going on to consider the charges that the transfer of educational responsibility should bring about in the lives of children in subnormality hospitals, it seems appropriate to look at the future as it is envisaged in the White Paper. The Wessex experiment has demonstrated what can be achieved in one region, Command 4683 outlines the changing approach and attitudes of society as a whole towards the mentally handicapped. Among the essential main principles which are stated in chapter 3 (pp. 9–10) of the report, occur the following:

1. The range of services in every area should be such that the family can be sure that their handicapped member will be properly cared for when it becomes necessary for him to leave the family home.

2. When a handicapped person has to leave his family home, temporarily or permanently, the substitute should be as homelike as possible, even if it is also a hospital. It should provide sympathetic and constant human relationships.

3. Hospital services for the mentally handicapped should be easily accessible to the population they serve. They should be associated with other hospital services so that a full range of specialist skills is easily available when needed for assessment and treatment.*

4. *Understanding and help from friends and neighbours and from the community at large are needed to help the family to maintain a normal social life and to give the handicapped member as nearly normal a life as his handicap or handicaps permit.*

These selected samples will serve to demonstrate vividly the total change from the old attitude of considering isolated custodial care for life as the best form of provision for the mentally handicapped.

The White Paper then goes on to critically examine and consider the present position and (p. 28) 'how far we are from applying fully the main principles on which services should be based'. It continues by describing in detail the 'component parts of the services we should now aim to provide' and means of achieving this aim. Most important in the context of this chapter is the stress that is placed on the need to make all forms of residential treatment as personalized and 'homelike' as possible, the need to preserve and maintain family and other personal relationships, the advantage in this respect of encouraging contact not only

* Compare the findings of the Wessex experiment.

with the immediate families but also with the local community.

The way ahead seems clear although the objectives cannot be achieved except over a long period of time, for apart from all financial considerations there is certainly evidence that these views are not universally held even by people at present giving devoted service in the hospitals. Nevertheless attitudes are changing and as the White Paper truly states (p. 19) there is now 'greater public awareness of and sympathy towards the mentally handicapped and their families and more open discussion of the subject and general expectation that the mentally handicapped should receive services of as high a quality as the state provides for any other group of disabled children or adults'.

Educational developments in the hospitals

The most immediate and, in many ways, radical change in the life of children living in subnormality hospitals and other institutions has come about in the field of education. Since the implementation of the Education (Handicapped Children) Act 1970 all children no matter how severe their physical or mental handicaps come within the scope of the educational system. This has meant that all hospital schools have ceased to be the responsibility of the hospital boards and more importantly both that their provision is now obligatory and also that they have to conform with all the accepted standards. In addition consideration must be given to all the children who were previously left without any form of education or stimulus. The consequences are widespread, from the financial angle, the hospitals gain, since not only are they relieved of the costs of providing staff and equipping the schools but they also receive rent from the education authorities for every part of their premises which are used for educational purposes. The money thus saved will be a fairly substantial sum, which should help in part at least to finance improvements in other aspects of the children's lives. A more important consequence is the sharing of responsibility for the children, educational decisions will now be properly made by educationalists, supported by all the ancillary services. The task facing the educational authorities is a formidable one and one that was initially made even more difficult by the fact that so little information or directives were supplied to them by the Department of Education and Science until a relatively late date before the transfer. An indication of the complexity of the situation and the way in which the authorities set about dealing with this new responsibility can be gained from the following example.

The hospital concerned is a large and comprehensive one in the Greater London Area. Its siting and physical features are good and the Management Committee have always been active and forward thinking. It would be true to say that its standards of care have been the best possible within the limits imposed by the resources that were available. The local authority had always been responsible for one of the two schools on the hospital site, the other, that for the mentally handicapped, had been provided by the hospital. In all, the hospital (which is for children only) provides for 726 patients, 340 of these are mentally handicapped. The other 386 suffer from other forms of illnesses both acute and chronic. Except for those too ill to attend school or to be taught on the wards, education was provided for all this second group of children. The same was not true of the first group. In January 1972, 339 children were concerned; of these fifty were aged sixteen and over, thirteen of this older group attended the school (which could only contain a maximum of eighty children), the other thirty-seven were not receiving any education. Of the younger children, 102 were receiving education (some part-time) and 187 were not. In other words at the time of transfer only one third of the children were being provided for.

These facts had been established and the school reorganized in the months subsequent to the transfer. Most of the children in the school had been attending it before the transfer, therefore the effect on their lives was not so dramatic as that on the other children, those who had previously been left without any provision whatever. The LEA had appointed as from 1 April 1971 a General Inspector/Adviser whose prime concern is the planning and reorganization of the educational services for the mentally handicapped, an appointment they would have liked to have been authorized to make at least six months earlier. Within a month, i.e. by May 1971, a series of case conferences attended by the Consultant Psychiatrist and other experts on the hospital staff, Nursing Staff, Local Authority Senior Officers from the Health and Education Departments and the Head and Deputy Head of the Hospital School had been initiated and are still being held at frequent intervals. At these conferences each child is being individually considered and fully discussed. The decision regarding his education is therefore being made in the light of all the available information. Incredibly by January 1972, sixty-nine children had already been considered in this way. In order to expedite matters ward visits were also made so that by the same date all the children concerned had been observed on several occasions and discussed with nursing and medical staff. The individual conferences will continue in the future but provisional plans have now been made for all the children and range from full attendance in the school, or until extensions to the school are built, in teaching groups either on or off the wards in which the children live, to providing the most severely affected children who require constant nursing care with the maximum educational stimulation possible. They will all be seen regularly by a teacher whose task this will be. The provision for all the children will be consistently reviewed and reassessed. The reports being presented to the local educational authority are full of a wealth of detailed planning for the future which will eventually totally revolutionize the children's lives, for it is correctly held that education for these children must be involved in every aspect of their lives and not just confined to the classroom and its activities. It is also quite obvious that an extremely good level of cooperation has already been achieved with the hospital authorities, who might well, had this not been the case, have rejected and perhaps resented many of the comments, criticisms and suggestions being made.

It would be wrong to pretend that problems do not sometimes arise at this early stage; basically all the premises used, for example, still belong to the hospital, the authority therefore can only suggest improvements they feel would be beneficial and then hopefully rely on the hospital being both willing and able to provide them from their limited resources. There are minor conflicts and some inter-professional prejudices still hold. There is still a body of expert and informed opinion which questions the feasibility of effecting really worthwhile improvements with the non-ambulant, incontinent severely retarded children. This is not unique to this hospital and something which will probably always remain a matter of personal opinion. 'Is it sensible to devote at least three years to achieve simply a responsive smile and freer head movement?' 'Should one accept that there is a level of retardation below which the results achieved do not justify the time, money and skilled service spent on gaining them?' On the other hand 'Is it potentially too dangerous to impose a new cut-off point?' These are valid questions. The present decision is that attempts should be made to help all children and certainly from the evidence I have seen in the hospital discussed above and others I have visited the task is being attempted with imagination, professional skill, energy and goodwill on the part of all concerned.

Hostel provision
White Paper

Some part of the problems of development and reorganization of the hospitals discussed so far should be alleviated as the local authorities step up their provision of hostels for those of the mentally handicapped who are capable of living in this way in the community. To the present there has been very little development of this service, presumably because insufficient time has elapsed since the Social Service Departments were set up. Priority, until the transfer of education responsibility, seems to have been given to improving the training centres. As the hostel provision does increase, so the hospital population should decrease and it is emphasized that, as is recommended for the hospitals, the population of the hostels should be drawn from the neighbourhood in which they are sited. An interesting observation has been made in one of the authorities where hostels are being set up. Some are for children who go daily to school from them and some for older people. Where the hostels are placed in old-established communities which tend to have a predominance of older families it has been far more difficult to awaken community interest and to achieve real acceptance than it has proved to be on the new housing estates. The reason seems to be two-fold; firstly that there is some resentment and fear of possible effects of this form of intrusion into a settled way of life and secondly, more interestingly, that the younger people on the new estates have in many cases had first-hand knowledge of the mentally handicapped, since many of them had worked in a voluntary capacity in the centres and hospitals during the latter part of their school or college life. This fact has increased their readiness to accept, rather than reject or fear the mentally handicapped living in their midst and fortunately it is becoming more common for the older children and students to have this kind of experience. We have been fortunate enough at the Lindens to be visited and helped by local schoolchildren in the last few years and there is no doubt whatever that the practice has been very beneficial to all concerned. It seems only fair however to strike a note of warning the other way, for it does seem to me that if we wish the community to welcome the mentally handicapped we have an absolute duty to help them to conform to the socially acceptable standards. For example I pass daily a large hospital whose patients do pass in and out freely and I have frequently seen them just stopping and going to the lavatory as the need took them. In this sort of case it is quite easy to understand why there is a strong body of neighbourhood opinion that 'the poor things should be locked up' since it must be difficult for mothers, for example, to explain to their young children why apparently grown men and women are doing something which they are being taught to think wrong.

The White Paper envisages that in the future the local authorities will have developed their services to the point where it is possible 'to fix for each area as early a date as possible after which the hospitals will not be asked to admit any more people who need residential rather than hospital care' (Command 4683, p. 56). It goes on to say that this may well take anything from fifteen to twenty years over the country as a whole. Nevertheless it is clearly the intention, at least of this present Conservative Government, that it will be achieved in the fastest possible time.

In this chapter the lives led by the children in the residential institutions have been discussed. On the whole their mental level is such that education in its truest and widest sense should be involved in every facet of their lives and not be just something that takes place in the school or training centre. There is no escaping the clear evidence that, at present, the lives these children lead are grossly deficient (a) in supplying their emotional needs (b) in providing social and language training and (c) in providing a stimulating environment which will enable them to develop to their full potential. Many studies, such as the one carried out by Ann and A. D. B. Clark,[10] show that children subjected to unstimulating environments become even further handicapped. No child should have to be admitted to a mental subnormality hospital simply because there is nowhere else for him to go. Wider provisions in the community, such as day nursery schools, etc., could avoid the admission of many more patients, especially the very young. Many more hostels should be provided and hospitals should be used only for those who need medical and nursing care.

In fairness it must be said that the hospitals themselves are in agreement, on the whole. For example, Dr Spencer, the Medical Director of Westwood Hospital, Bradford, says, 'Scrutiny of case histories reveals that the referral ... for hospital care is often the bottom of a ladder of rejection.' And again,

Patients stay in hospital today not because the hospital authorities wish to detain them but because nobody else wants them and they have nowhere else to go. ... Ideally, if the hospitals could be relieved of overcrowding and improved in effectiveness, they would be able to train patients to a standard more acceptable for community care. To this end the development of special units within hospitals for investigation, assessment and the treatment of spastics, autistic children and psychopaths, for example, is a progressive step (p. 5).[11]

Meanwhile, every attempt should be made to modify the present pattern of ward life. In a personal discussion of this, Kushlick made the interesting suggestion that this might happen more quickly if it was not initiated, as it usually is at present, at ward level, but from the top. In other words the conviction should come from the administrative level and filter down to the wards. At present anyone initiating it in any other way inevitably comes into conflict with age-old traditions and principles which he totally lacks the authority to alter radically. My own experiences would fully support this suggestion and comment. The actual schools and training centres have not been described in this chapter. This is not because they have no importance but because they form part of the pattern of all training centres which will be fully discussed in the following chapter.

Chapter Four
Training Schools

Training schools

In the late eighteenth century the Industrial Revolution altered the whole structure of the country's economy and way of life. It was during this period also that social legislation, inspired by the great humanitarians such as Lord Shaftesbury, really began. The passing of the Education Act of 1870 provided for universal compulsory education. In 1899 the Education (Defective Children) Act first gave permissive powers to the local education authorities to provide schools and classes for children 'who, not being imbecile and not merely dull and backward, are, by reason of mental and physical defect, incapable of receiving proper benefit from instruction in ordinary schools.' Public attitudes towards the care and treatment of the feeble-minded and mentally ill were growing progressively more humane.

In early days, simple-minded idiots were generally tolerated as part of a local community. From the reign of Edward II onwards, they were distinguished from the mentally ill, the 'born fools', being given legal status as wards of the king while the mentally ill were regarded with much less tolerance and either persecuted as possessed by witches or left to roam about uncared for. It was only after the Reformation that this distinction was blurred: both the idiots and the mentally sick were herded together and often cruelly treated, since they were regarded as being responsible for their own state.

During the nineteenth century, the main emphasis was on custodial care. The greater awareness of the problems of mental deficiency, as distinct from mental illness, led to the formation of many voluntary bodies which ultimately joined together after the passing of the Mental Deficiency Act of 1913 to form the Central Association for Mental Welfare. In 1964, this Association amalgamated with the Child Guidance Council and the National Council for Mental Hygiene to form the National Association for Mental Health. The Mental Deficiency Act of 1913 was still heavily weighted in favour of segregation and custodial care, but it did formulate definitions of the different grades of mental defectiveness which were only replaced by the Mental Health Act of 1959. These definitions were as follows.

Idiots were 'persons in whose case there exists mental defectiveness of such degree that they are unable to guard themselves against common physical dangers.'

Imbeciles were 'persons in whose case there exists mental defectiveness which, though not amounting to idiocy, is yet so pronounced that they are incapable of managing themselves or their affairs or, in the case of children, of being taught to do so.'

The *feeble-minded* were defined as

persons in whose case there exists mental defectiveness which though not amounting to imbecility is yet pronounced sufficiently for them to require supervision and control or, in the case of children, that they appear to be permanently incapable by reason of such defectiveness of receiving proper benefit from the instruction in ordinary schools.

This Act excluded all children who were idiots or imbeciles from schools. The feeble-minded were not excluded unless they presented problems of behaviour and management. The duty of ascertaining such children and reporting them to the mental deficiency committees rested with the certifying medical officers and the school medical officers (the problems and defects of this procedure will be discussed later). Once a child had been so ascertained, he was dealt with by statutory supervision under Section 57 of the Act. In other words, he was visited at three-monthly intervals by a statutory officer. This meant, in the majority of cases, that these children remained at home in the sole care of their parents. Only if the child was shown to be neglected or cruelly treated was custodial care recommended. The good parent was therefore given little help or relief, for there was no provision for any form of training for these children.

It was to help relieve the burden borne by these parents that voluntary enterprise encouraged by the Central Association for Mental Welfare initiated the first centres aimed at training the defectives living in the community. These early training centres

were created at the end of the First World War and had to cope
with poor accommodation, lack of funds and, perhaps most
important of all, lack of any kind of trained personnel. The work
in the London area was begun because of 'the vision and enterprise of a single enthusiast' (pp. 11–23).[1] Immediately after the
end of the War, in 1919, Elfrida Rathbone opened the Lilian
Greg centre in a dingy room in a poverty stricken area at Kings
Cross. At first she had one helper and funds were provided by
herself and some personal friends. For the first two years the
centre was attended by ten low-grade 'ineducable children'. During the following years voluntary associations established centres
in about fifteen towns and counties. Most of these centres were
only open for a few sessions during the week. They catered
chiefly for the older boys and girls in whatever premises could be
found. Nevertheless, the 1922 Annual Report of the Board of
Control stated:

On all sides we hear how greatly these centres are appreciated by the
parents and how much easier it has become to gain their confidence
when their children are in attendance. We anticipate that the regular
occupation and training afforded by this form of supervision will
tend to decrease the number of cases who will ultimately have to be
sent to an institution.

In 1923, the Board empowered local authorities to apply for
grants to support the centres, although it still expected that the
centres should be opened by the voluntary societies and only in
exceptional circumstances by the local authorities. One important
step forward was the passing of the 1927 Amendment of the 1913
Act. Local authorities were now obliged to make provision for
the training and occupation of defectives as well as for supervision. Following this there was a steady growth in the number
of occupation centres, although it was interrupted and badly
affected by the Second World War.

In 1959 the Mental Health Act was passed. This Act not only
made it compulsory, subject to various conditions and limitations, for all severely subnormal children to receive training
either at home or in a centre, but also redefined the terms of the
1913 Act, substituting 'severely subnormal' for 'imbecile' and
'idiot', and 'subnormal' for 'feeble-minded' (for the definitions
of these terms see chapter 3 pp. 46–7). It also stated that the

severely subnormal should no longer be deemed ineducable and incapable of being educated at school but instead 'unsuitable for education at school'. The name of the centres was changed from occupation to training centres as a more accurate description of their functions. By 1967 it was claimed 92 per cent of children under sixteen (excluding those in the subnormality hospitals) and 82 per cent of those over sixteen were receiving some form of training either in centres or at home, the under-sixteens at junior training centres, the older ones at senior training centres or sheltered workshops.

These facts and figures reflect the tremendous energy, drive and achievements of all the people and agencies who had fought so hard to effect improvements in the care and education of the mentally handicapped. It was not until July 1970 when the Education (Handicapped Children) Act received the Royal Assent, however, that the statutory right to education within the educational system was given to these children. It became effective on 1 April 1971. At last there was an 'end to isolation' for from that date 'No child, within the age limits of education therefore, will be outside the scope of the educational system' (DES Circular, p. 13).

Problems at the date of transfer

There were two separate groups of problems at the date of the transfer of responsibility for the Junior Training Schools, one of which could perhaps have been avoided, the second the legacy of the previous system.

To consider the first group, on all sides it is common to hear that the local authorities wished that they could have had much more official information at an earlier date, to enable them to start the necessary planning and investigations in accordance with official policy. It was not until 22 September 1970 that Circular 15/70 was sent out 'To Local Education Authorities and certain other bodies'.[2] Clause 2 states 'The purpose of this circular is to provide local education authorities with information and guidance to assist their planning in the coming months and in particular to draw their attention to steps which need to be taken before the assumption of this new educational responsibility.' This at the end of September with the effective date of the transfer six months away, i.e. 1 April 1971! This would have been little enough time if the people concerned had had no other work to do and if authorization had been given to employ the Special Inspector/Organizers from the time that planning began. Neither of these things happened so the task was colossal, for in those few months they were: 1. To take the necessary steps in cooperation with the local health authorities and hospital authorities to ensure a smooth transfer; 2. To obtain full information about the existing arrangements in their area; 3. To establish which of the services in their own area they were to assume responsibility for and to forward detailed information of each centre or unit to serve as a proposal for the Secretary of State's approval no later than 30 November, in other words in *two months* only.

They had also to discover and establish the needs of all the children of school age not attending any of the centres. In addition they were 'advised' to familiarize themselves with new building projects currently being planned and 'encouraged' to begin considering their long-term policy concerning the special education of mentally handicapped children. The authorities deserve great credit for all that they did actually achieve of these objectives in the time allotted.

The second problem in this group was the amount of totally unnecessary anxiety which, through lack of information again, was aroused in the staffs of the schools, particularly the large number of untrained teachers. There is no doubt whatever that they felt threatened and needed convincing that the authorities were in fact on their side and not considering ways in which to dispose of them. Here again many of the authorities made great efforts to alleviate this situation by holding meetings; unfortunately though, these meetings did not always achieve their purpose since they could give no official answers to the crucial questions. The qualified staff did know some months before what their position, status and salary were likely to be but in some cases the unqualified staff only knew two days before the date of transfer. Two separate Head Teachers of schools in different areas made the identical comment to me 'It got the whole thing off on the wrong foot.'

The second group of problems at the time of transfer were the direct consequence of the inadequacy of the existing provision. In all directions there were shortages. Perhaps the most vital in terms of integrating the service into an educational system which requires professional training for all its teaching staff was the gross shortage of qualified teachers. Secondly there was a shortage of available places, e.g. in 1969, of the children who were considered suitable for placement in training centres (as they then were) 1800 were on waiting lists; this figure does not, of course, include the younger children since there was an even greater shortage of nursery class provision, or those children who were left at home for such reasons as severe physical handicaps or behaviour disorders. Thirdly there was a shortage of suitable or even reasonable buildings and fourthly of residential provision to enable children who lived too far away from such centres as there were to attend on a daily basis. Perhaps it should be stressed that there was a wide variation between the different local authorities: some had made excellent and adequate provision, others totally inadequate and poor provision. The consequences of this on the resources of the education authorities taking over are obvious.

The question of the status, qualifications and salaries of the teachers was resolved by an official decision, which, in effect, accepted the inevitable fact that for an interim period the service would have to continue to be run with a large number of unqualified teachers. On 1 April 1971 all staff whose primary function was teaching were automatically transferred to the service of the education authorities, not necessarily the case with the non-teaching staff. It was also specifically laid down (and the pity was that it was not made known earlier) that all the transferred staff should have terms and conditions of employment not less favourable than those they enjoyed at the time of transfer. Two consequences arose from this decision, first that the service could continue without a break; second this is, and will be, a potential source of friction within the staffrooms as long as it persists, that in all schools teachers are employed with different salaries and status, although involved in the same capacity with the children. This situation is complicated enough but the fact that one of the first moves of many authorities was to appoint classroom assistants tends to make it even more so. For example one relatively uncomplicated school has for its staff one Burnham trained teacher who has, of course, total equality of salary and status with all other teachers so qualified, six teachers who hold the Training Council Diploma but whose years of experience vary, therefore some will be regarded as fully qualified before the others, two teachers seconded at the time of transfer to study for the Training Council Diploma, three unqualified teachers who, if they had remained employed by the Health Department, would automatically have been seconded in their turn to follow such a course, since their responsible authority operated a training scheme (which, incidently has been a casualty of the transfer) and three non-teaching classroom assistants. In other schools the position is even more complicated and since the training centres are now schools a further source of jealousy and friction arises from the fact that there are some graded posts within the schools which normally are given to qualified staff. Frequently these are the younger, more recently appointed members. It is easy to understand how this can affect the older people whose years of poorly rewarded work have for all their inadequacies provided a service which demonstrated that something could be done with and for these children and which also laid down the groundwork of experience from which all else is developing.

In time these problems should disappear, for the official intention is that the training of teachers of mentally handicapped children shall 'as soon as possible' (and one hopes there is not a faintly ominous hint about this qualification) be integrated into the normal teacher-training system and that after this has taken place, such teachers will have fully qualified status on appointment. In the interim, teachers holding the present Diploma can take a year's conversion course which gives them full qualified status, or attain it after five years teaching experience subsequent to their gaining the Diploma. It is not intended to appoint any more unqualified staff as teachers but it is intended to continue for a period both the two-year and one-year courses leading to the Training Council Diploma for 'those for whom the three year course is not appropriate'. Presumably this means for those who do not have sufficient 'O'-Level passes to be accepted into a College of Education. It may well be that at the present juncture there is no alternative if the schools are to be adequately staffed but it does seem that there is a possible danger of the 'limited period' spoken of persisting for a very long time with the consequent persistence of staff inequality.

The shortage of places and of residential provision can only be remedied in part as the shortage of teachers becomes less acute but, of course, buildings are also essential. The existing buildings were automatically transferred to the education authorities on the allotted date, together with the resources already allocated by the Department of Health and Social Security for approved building plans. After this initial period however, any future plans will have to be submitted as part of the authorities' special school-building programmes. In this may lie a source of delay which was predicted by some critics of the decision to transfer responsibility. Local authorities never receive approval to proceed with *all* their major building plans, in other words the needs of the mentally handicapped will have to be weighed against the equally pressing needs of other handicapped children, instead of being, as previously, the sole concern of one department. The sums involved are not small and will be proportionally larger according to the adequacy or not of the transferred premises. Since all the buildings will have to conform as quickly as possible to the standards laid down for other schools, some areas where little or no provision was previously made will be faced with the task of submitting major building schemes for years to come, unless special funds are somehow made available to meet this need.

The costs of the service have also increased substantially in other ways. Firstly the salary bills have gone up in every school, as the scales have all been increased to bring them nearer to those paid in other schools, and also since in nearly every school it has been found necessary to increase the numbers of teaching and non-teaching staff. This item alone accounts for an increased annual cost in one typical hospital school of roughly £12,000 a year and of over £6000 in a typical junior training school. The salary charge to the education department is also increased by the need to appoint more administrative and advisory officers since the expanded Social Services Departments were unable to release and transfer officers previously employed in this branch of the service. As one administrative officer commented to me, 'To bring these services up to the required standards is going to cost a lot of money'. The vital question is 'where will it come from?' Circular 15/70 (section 22 page 7) somewhat optimistically talks about local authorities deciding what funds should be transferred for the purpose from *within their own budgets* and offsetting expended costs in one department by savings in another. But apart from all else this seems totally to overlook the fact that there is now a statutory obligation to enlarge and expand the service and to make provision for many children previously left out. There just isn't the money available to the local authorities from 'within their own budgets'.

Consequences of the transfer

In recent months I have been getting opinions in various ways and from many sources of the consequences of the transfer, and some of these are quoted below.

I don't like it all, the parents have been 'sold a pup' (Administrative Officer).

It is quite unkind and unrealistic to pretend that education can by some form of magic radically alter these children (Medical Officer).

At the moment there seems to have been little change for all practical purposes. We realize that staff cannot be trained overnight, but do hope that our children will not be the 'poor relation' of the education system (parent).

Since the change-over we have not been aware of any change in the education of our child (parent).

Since the change-over there seems to be more money available for books and equipment and for educational outings, etc. (parent).

In the educational field it is certain that at grass-roots level the challenge (of the change) is being accepted. There is a marked enthusiasm among teachers and organizers to get to grips with the new task of teaching the mentally handicapped, to explore new methods and look for new guide-lines. ...

There is a challenge however to those who plan and those who administer the education service to do more than change the label on the gate to realize the special needs of their new handicapped protégées and not think they can get away with it on the cheap. Slight modification of the present special education provision will not do and the new pupils must not become Cinderellas (*The Challenge of*

Change, Annual Report 1971 National Society for Mentally Handicapped Children).[3]

Nothing but good has come from the transfer: financially we are better off in every way. It was morally wrong to exclude children from the system so now this has ended the parents are much happier. They are finding it much easier to get support and interested advice, for it does seem that most paediatricians are very poor at relationships with parents. The Teachers' Centre is now open to all my teachers and they are finding it a marvellous source for collecting information and providing opportunities for meeting and discussing with other teachers, etc. We now have a yearly assessment meeting too, which is attended by Medical Officers of Health, heads of the nearby Special School, social workers and psychologists. We feel we really belong (head teacher).

It is wonderful to know how much I can spend every year on the children, before I was just told to ask for what I wanted, so I never asked for very much because I thought they would cut it down and stop something I really needed if I did (head teacher).

It was sad how the authorities had to go out of their way to meet the people involved to get the message over that they were on their side. We have arranged many meetings and are setting up as soon as possible and as many as possible 'In Service Courses of Training'. They are very well attended. We have opened up the Teachers' Centre to these new teachers and they obviously appreciate it enormously. (Note this is a different authority from the one in which the Head Teacher quoted above works). We are anxious to have the funds to employ another psychologist because we are beginning to question whether the present psychological assessments are really satisfactory (Inspector Organizer).

Morale-wise the benefit has been enormous. We now really feel members of a profession and do appreciate the courses being organized. As teachers we have benefited in every way and so have the children. Salaries are better, the classes are smaller. We are much more generously equipped and as a Head who is now invited to take part in discussions on the children on terms of equal status with the Doctors, Senior Nursing Staff, Psychologists, Social Workers I feel much more than ever before that the value of an education opinion given by an educationalist is being accepted and not considered at the bottom of the file (head teacher of a school in a hospital).

It is wonderful that I can now and with the support of my local authority implement in the school the ideas and plans I have formed over my years of experience with the children. Previously the hospital was the supreme authority and I had to seek permission for every little thing (head teacher of a school in a hospital).

I feel that overall the Local Authorities have given a good deal of thought to the transfer. I am sure that in the course of time our children will benefit considerably and even at the end of one year in many instances one can see a change of atmosphere and attitude. This is especially noticeable in the old junior training centres, where the attitude was minding rather than teaching, or where the staff were not allowed to teach as they would wish. The help of advisers has been particularly profitable and there is no doubt that the staff was very encouraged by the support and help which is now available to them (Joyce McCarthy, E. Midlands Regional Officer NSMHC in *Parents Voice*).[4]

1 April 1971 started at Woodlands with a telephone call from our Chief Education Officer, welcoming us under Education's umbrella and giving us his assurance that the authority would do everything in their power to help us make the new regime as successful as possible. . . .

The same morning the white-capped, white-overalled school meals service staff absorbing our own dinner assistant, busied themselves preparing the dining tables and serving the meal. So the first practical changes were soon felt.

No longer in isolation we can benefit from calling on other disciplines, one example of which is the Physical Education Officer, or we are able to consult with Heads of other Special Schools and make contact with teachers in schools and at the Teachers' Centre.

No doubt there will be disappointments and being part of a larger organization has its disadvantages but I feel confident in reassuring parents that every endeavour will be made to overcome these as they occur and that effort will continue to be made in order to prepare our children for a better future (Headmistress of Woodland School Blackpool in *Parents Voice*).[5]

It is hoped that 'Education' intends to maintain the specialized status of these MHC Schools, and their staffs, with the minimum of 'cross infection' from their normal schools (parent).

Our pipe dream. Perhaps at some future date our children could be allowed to share some of the educational facilities (or even classes) of the normal schools in the area! (parent).

One of the nicest things since the transfer has been that the head teacher at the local Primary School and I have been able to carry out a long cherished idea. Our children now share some classes, we sometimes go to them, they sometimes come to us. In Music and Movement for instance a child from the Primary School has as a partner one of our children. They get on famously together, and are now going for little trips together. It is wonderful how our children look forward to it and how much brighter they seem and how much better they talk during these shared lessons (headteacher).

The work of the training schools

The purpose of the training schools is to develop the full potentialities of the children who attend them in an environment which satisfies their need for acceptance and security and which gives them the possibility of achievement, while at the same time taking account of their different levels of development.

The children who attend the schools have been described by Professor Gunzburg as follows:

Emotionally they are very young and therefore have the emotional needs of young children. ... Intellectually they are in the pre-school stage and formal educational work is therefore very often completely inappropriate. Physically they are often more advanced than in the other two aspects, though even there, they may lag considerably behind the stage reached by their contemporary. Socially their handicaps have very often resulted in considerable under-achievement, partly because of inadequate training, partly because of over-protection, and partly because of lack of encouragement and consequent feelings of insecurity.

Professor Gunzburg delineates four major areas of training and education: self-help, communication, socialization and occupation.

Professor Tizard, in the Brooklands experiment described in chapter 3, stresses the vital necessity of development of speech and its inseparability from the total programme of education and care of the children. He also points out the need to adjust one's standards so as to be able to take due account of a mentally handicapped child's emotional immaturity when one is confronted by his physical size.

It is now becoming the common practice in training teachers to base the theoretical approach to child development on Jean Piaget's work on the learning processes of children and his four stages of cognitive development. These are, very briefly:

1. The sensorimotor stage during which the child learns to co-ordinate his actions with the knowledge he receives through his perceptions and begins to assemble the information he is gaining into a rudimentary framework of reference. In a normal child this stage usually lasts up to about the age of two.

2. The pre-operational stage during which the child begins to use the different forms of symbolic media such as pictures, words and numbers. He is constantly enlarging and enriching his rudimentary framework of perceptions by the use of such things as imaginative play, active experimenting and questions. This stage usually lasts until the mental age of about six.

3. The concrete operational stage during which the child begins to develop concepts of conservation of matter, length, weight and volume, and to deal efficiently with the materials and properties of the world around him. This stage is usually fully achieved by about the mental age of eleven.

4. The formal operational stage during which the child moves into adolescence and develops his capacity to hypothesize from experience and to develop abstract concepts.

Since the functioning intelligence quotient of the severely sub-normal is rarely above 55, it is clear that their cognitive development will not often progress beyond Piaget's second stage. In addition, some of them will, in fact, only begin to reach this second stage when, according to their chronological age, they are ready to leave the junior training school if the age limits at the school are adhered to.

The functions of training

If we accept Piaget's theory, it follows that the work in the junior training schools should provide the child with the experience and materials suitable to his developmental stage. All training should be presented in finely graded steps which the child can comprehend at any one time.

Professor Tizard argues that this provision and the development and encouragement of the use of speech should arise naturally both from the situations presented in the normal activities of every day life and from opportunities carefully planned both inside and outside the classroom. He sees as fundamental to this the development of happy relationships both with adults and other children. He does not favour formal speech therapy since it might tend to place emphasis on the manner of speech rather than encouraging the desire to communicate verbally. Gunzburg, on the other hand, while also stressing the vital importance of speech development, advocates the incorporation of special exercises to train the children in certain aspects of speech.

The actual situation

Although scientific study and assessment of the application of this theoretical approach is almost totally lacking, two interesting papers have been published recently which have attempted such an assessment. The first, by P. F. Simpson in 1967, stresses the crucial importance of the formulation of sound and clearly expressed aims.[6] From the survey he has conducted and the visits he has carried out to a large number of centres over a period of five years, he states: 'Patently, it is obvious to a trained educationist that aims, both general and specific, are conspicuous by their absence throughout large areas of the training centre world.' He then quotes the following examples of attempts by different heads to define their aims: 'Oh well, we believe in free activity'; 'To keep them happily occupied'; 'To train them so that they can do a job'; 'As long as the little dears are gaily occupied, then I know that I am doing the right thing.' He concludes that although they may all contain a grain of truth, these aims are hardly adequate, as they stand, as a basis on which to design a programme of education or training.

He then examines and analyses some of the training centre time-tables in current use and finds that a substantial part of each day is frequently spent on such things as:

1. Registration, sometimes carried out in a general assembly, where 100 children have to answer when their name is called.

2. Assembly, where over thirty minutes can be spent each day with all the children in the 'hall' on an 'act of worship'.

3. Personal hygiene – at set intervals all the children, whether continent or not, are lined up to be toileted. One might add in passing that the more one investigates the lives of severely subnormal children the larger the shadow of the toilet seems to loom.

The ability to use it is still often a condition for admission to some training schools. To me it is quite incomprehensible why, when children are toilet trained, they are not allowed to go to the lavatory by themselves when they need to do so.

An earlier analysis of training school time-tables carried out by Norris in 1961 supports Simpson's findings.[7] Norris found that children aged five to nine, all of whom had mental ages of under five, spent 14 per cent of their time on resting, 24 per cent on register, assembly, etc., and 22 per cent on eating and going to the lavatory. This left only 40 per cent of their time for lessons and play. Only 17 per cent of this time was spent on free play, the rest was spent on group activities and sedentary lesson periods – activities which were quite inappropriate for children of this mental age.

Although in the primary schools the whole pattern of short periods of subject teaching is now considered out of date and constricting to both children and teachers alike, nevertheless Simpson commonly found meticulously drawn up time-tables in use in the junior training schools. The time-tabled subjects included English, sums, social training, i.t.a., knitting, nursery rhymes, modelling with clay – each period lasting twenty to thirty minutes. He concludes that much of the content of these time-tables is inessential and inappropriate to the children's needs.

The second survey, by Anne Marshall, studied the effectiveness of training for the mentally subnormal in junior training schools.[8] The aim of this survey is well described in the foreword by Ruth Rees Thomas.

The National Association for Mental Health has been aware of the lack of trained observation and assessment of the real educational needs of children in junior training centres.... Accordingly in 1963 the NAMH appointed a psychologist, Miss Anne Marshall, to undertake a limited survey of the competence and achievements of boys and girls in the upper age range of junior training centres in three different areas of England. This age group was chosen in order to study the effect of their training over the maximum period and to make it possible to predict with greater confidence whether these children would be able to adjust to adult life in the community (p. 1).

That this survey was initiated and financed by the NAMH is an interesting example of the vital role that this and other voluntary societies, such as the National Society for Mentally Handicapped and the Invalid Children's Aid Association, still play. It is true to say that all the improvements in every sphere, from providing services to educating public and official opinion, are directly due to the pioneering work of these and similar organizations.

The areas chosen for the survey were:

1. A small industrial area combined with a small town and rural district of south-west England.
2. A large industrial area in the Midlands.
3. A large industrial area in north-western England.

In all, 165 children were seen in nineteen schools; ninety-eight boys and sixty-seven girls. There were fifty-five children seen in each of the main areas. Anne Marshall points out that the findings of this survey do not necessarily represent a national average. Nevertheless, the areas selected are good examples of three types of locality frequently found in the country as a whole.

By use of standardized tests, the children's achievement was measured and related to their mental capacity, to various factors in the environment, to symptoms of maladjustment, to the various causes of the subnormality, and to the number of years spent in the junior training schools. The results, therefore, give a comprehensive picture of the children's achievement.

What the survey has not attempted is any assessment of the effect on achievement of a very great number of such variable factors as the different facilities available at each school, the size of the centre, its location, the number of trained staff, the effect of changes of staff or policy, etc. These variable factors are of the utmost importance and there is a vital need for more research to assess their effect on the children's achievements. For example, 29 per cent of the staff in all the schools held the NAMH diploma and in 53 per cent of the centres the supervisor was qualified. However, when these over-all figures are broken down, it is shown that the location of the school affects not only the type and size of accommodation provided but also the number of qualified staff working in it. Whereas in the suburban schools 28 per cent of the staff and 60 per cent of the supervisors were qualified, in the country schools this was only the case for 17 per cent of the staff and 20 per cent of the supervisors. Similarly, of the ten suburban schools, six were purpose-built, two were pre-fabricated or converted houses and two were in hired premises. By contrast, three of the five country schools were in hired premises, one only was purpose-built, and one was held in a pre-fabricated or converted house. Hired premises usually provide unsatisfactory accommodation which make large classes inevitable, since they are frequently halls which cannot be subdivided. From these two examples of the variable factors, it follows that the children in the least satisfactory premises also have the greatest chance of being taught by unqualified teachers.

The attainments of the children as revealed by the survey must, therefore, only be regarded as a statement of what has been achieved by children aged fourteen to fifteen at the time when the survey was carried out. They may not in any way reflect the potential achievement of such children; a great deal more research over a period of years will be necessary before it will be possible to come to any accurate conclusions as regards the relationship between actual and potential achievement.

The skills of the children in the four areas formulated by Gunzburg – self-help, communication, socialization and occupation – were assessed by means of his progress assessment chart. By far the highest percentage scores were attained in the area of self-help, the average being 84 per cent. Socialization came next with an average of 57 per cent; for occupation the score was 55 per cent and for communication 46 per cent. This is a disquieting result particularly since, as stated previously, authorities such as Tizard and Gunzburg stress the vital importance of the development of language skills. Tizard's Brooklands experiment showed that a good level of success in this area could be achieved with severly subnormal children who had also been hospitalized for a period of years.

A closer inspection of the results shows that there are very low scores in certain items of even the most successful area, and that these low scores relate to achievements which would have a great deal of relevance to the child's ability to function in the normal community. For example, 22 per cent of the children were still not capable of walking up and down stairs one foot to a stair and 10 per cent could not even achieve this with both feet together on one step. (The most severely physically handicapped children were not included in the percentages.) Even more significant in the same area is the fact that only 38 per cent could move about the neighbourhood unsupervised and cross the streets. It is possible that this percentage should be higher since a number of cases were marked as 'no opportunity' or 'not known', but even allowing for this the score is very low. The same qualification must be made about the accuracy of the scores for other skills. Nevertheless, these scores are still very low and the skills are of importance for assessing the child's prospects of coping in the community. In the area of socialization, for example, the following scores were obtained:

Goes on simple errands outside the house	32 per cent
Is trusted with money or errands	23 per cent
Goes to shop and fetches specified items	24 per cent
Answers the telephone	6 per cent
Uses pencil for recognizable drawings	55 per cent
Uses tools, kitchen utensils, garden tools	30 per cent
Cuts very carefully round outlines	24 per cent

All the skills involving motor control have low scores; the average percentage is only 44. In this area also the Brooklands experiment demonstrated that these abilities could be developed.

In the area of communication all the average scores, with the exception of colour recognition and naming, are low. For 'money' the score was 21 per cent and for 'reading age of seven years or over' 7 per cent. These results are, perhaps, understandable in view of the children's basic intelligence, but the following are less so:

Refers correctly to morning and afternoon	57 per cent
Tells left from right on himself	40 per cent
Adds pennies and halfpennies	13 per cent
Gives change out of a shilling	19 per cent
Understands difference between day–week, minute–hours, etc.	21 per cent

A communication check test was devised and administered by the investigator to evaluate the teacher's assessments as marked on the progress assessment chart. The difference between the two was only significant on a very few items which related to the children's performance in such things as 'telling the time to a quarter of an hour'. This check test is equally illuminating for we find in it such items as the following:

Knows traffic lights (red for stop – green for go)	43 per cent
Knows the day	58 per cent
Knows the month	26 per cent
Knows own birthday (day and month)	24 per cent
Knows age	62 per cent
Knows address	50 per cent
Addresses envelope to himself	5 per cent

It seems fair to conclude that, on this evidence, very few, if any, of these children would be able to function in the normal community without constant supervision and support. It therefore seems necessary to re-plan the pattern of training in these junior schools so that the children's needs are better supplied. It is true that this is already being done in the more advanced schools. I have visited some where the difference in verbal ability and body poise and control is quite marked between the older children in the school whose training in the earlier years followed the old pattern and the younger ones, who have, from the beginning, been trained by qualified teachers using the new techniques.

This interesting and important survey raises other questions besides making helpful suggestions. To me, one of the most significant of the findings is that the children who had been in the school system until 1959 or later, i.e. throughout their primary school years, performed at a significantly higher level than the other children in every area and especially in communication. These children formed just over a quarter of the total sample and tended to be of normal or near normal appearance, although they did include some Mongols. In 45 per cent of these cases the cause of their subnormality was not known, but many of them had a large number of adverse factors in their background and their fathers were in unskilled or semi-skilled occupations. It is possible, therefore, that their subnormality was not simply pathological but was influenced by their poor environmental conditions and could therefore have been improved or prevented.

In spite of these qualifications it does seem reasonable to say that these children do seem to demonstrate some of the advantages we may expect, now that the education of all children has properly been made the responsibility of the Department of Education and Science.

To sum up from these researches and recent experiences there is now sufficient information to plan the initial development of work in the new training schools. There is evidence that the children will develop better if their day is modelled instead on the free-choice informal curriculum which is generally used in nursery schools. This type of activity should be coupled with a warm, accepting teacher–child relationship, which would help to develop and improve the child's motivation to learn, since he would then find the whole situation more enjoyable. The children should whenever possible be taken outside the school; they should be given as many opportunities as can be organized to learn to live in the world by practising in the real milieu. The classroom shop, for instance, should only be a stepping stone to going out to real shops. Learning about traffic lights in the centre should be followed by experience with the real thing. Playing with a toy telephone should lead the child, with encouragement and training, to answer and use a real one.

The more advanced schools are already demonstrating the soundness of these principles. Neil O'Connor and Beate Hermelin, in a series of carefully controlled experiments, have been able to formulate certain conclusions about the learning processes of these children. On the basis of their findings they have made some very practical suggestions which could be helpful when training programmes are being devised.[9]

The further education of severely subnormal children

There is space in this chapter only for a brief consideration of the further educational needs of severely subnormal children after the age of sixteen when they should be transferred from the junior training schools. Some of the more modern ones are flexible and, in fact, disregard the chronological age of the children. Instead they move them on when they appear to have reached the right level of maturation, which may be either earlier or later than sixteen. This system has many advantages but may not always be workable: if the school is small, there may not be room to retain them while at the same time admitting all the younger children who need places. The different levels of maturation in each child may also create problems since the older children may have reached or be reaching physical maturity and so require very different facilities and techniques of management.

It is now well known that maturation continues after the age of sixteen, so the severely subnormal can benefit from further training and education. The task of training them must inevitably be a lengthy one, probably extending beyond the teens and into the early twenties, because of their slow rate of learning. It is also now established that the measured IQ of the severely subnormal does not necessarily give an indication of his ability to carry out useful work which is commercially valuable. Other factors such as his motivation, personality, socialization and persistence are of equal importance. Some severely handicapped people will never be able to progress beyond the stage of being minded and occupied, while at the other extreme others will achieve relative independence within the community. Many more will be able to function competently in a sheltered environment or workshop.

It is generally accepted that there are three stages of development in the senior training centre, the first of which – the 'transition' stage – follows immediately after the move from the junior training centre or hospital school, and which may often be initiated before transfer. During this period, the development of adult skills, behaviour and work habits are actively taught and encouraged. The second 'sheltered environment' stage leads to a level of independent mobility and self-care and to a higher level of social functioning. This in turn leads to the final stage of potential relative independence.[10] Professor Gunzburg stresses the necessity for basing the whole pattern of training in the senior centres on the acquisition of greater language ability and of those skills which will be directly useful in living within the community – the ability to use transport to and from work, to dress correctly and appropriately, to understand what other people mean by time concepts such as 'a fortnight', and to shop and to budget to whatever extent is possible. He also suggests that the design of the centre should be geared to the conditions that the people attending them are likely to meet in real life. For example, over-excessive safeguards built into industrial machinery would be less beneficial than constant practice and training with a normally safeguarded machine. A kitchen fitted up completely with labour-saving gadgets is pointless because it is unrealistic. As Gunzburg says, 'Learning should be by doing, handling, manipulating and this must take place in the same kind of conditions as are commonly found outside the centre.' [10]

One of the most interesting developments of recent years has been the changeover from 'occupation' based on crafts such as weaving or basket and stool-making to workshops in which industrial machinery is set up and work is done under contract which satisfies the requirements of the contractor. By this means it is possible for the subnormal to achieve the satisfaction of earning money by his own efforts. Some of these workshops are being set up in mental subnormality hospitals, many are run by local authorities. One example of this is at Brighton where the sheltered workshop is actually on one floor of a large building which is otherwise let out to industrial firms. The people attending this workshop really feel that they are part of the working community for they go to work with everyone else, take the same lifts to their own 'firm', clock in and draw their wages in the same way. The supervisor of this centre described to me how the attitudes of the other workmen in the building had altered once they met and observed the mentally handicapped in daily contact. This was illustrated by their behaviour in the lifts: initially they tended to avoid being in a lift in which a group of the handicapped was travelling; now they travel with them without hesitation, chat en route, shout to them to 'come on' as they hold the lift door open. They are now actively interested and under the stimulus of this interest, encouragement and acceptance, the subnormals are both functioning on a higher social level and maturing more rapidly.

A very interesting pilot scheme was initiated by the National Society for the Mentally Handicapped when they opened their National Hospital and Training Centre in Slough in 1963. The purpose of this experiment was to demonstrate to the community at large that a large percentage of mentally handicapped children could, given appropriate care and training, take their place in the open community to some extent. At the same time, research was undertaken to discover the best training methods.

The Centre consists of two villas which each provide accommodation for fifteen severely handicapped young men and women aged between sixteen and twenty-six. Twenty others attend daily and share the use of the adjacent training centre and works canteen. In the latter the trainees learn by daily practice how to conduct themselves in this situation. They are also trained to cope with the basic problems of transportation, the use of money and verbal communication, which includes the correct use of the telephone. Simultaneously, an investigation is carried out in the well-equipped workshop to discover the most suitable work for each trainee as a prelude to training them to do it. The trainees are referred to the unit by their own local authority, which also pays the costs of those selected to go there.

This centre has been an outstanding success and now forms the model for other authorities wishing to set up similar facilities. Since it was opened it has completed the training of forty-seven young men and women. Of these, about one in four have reacted sufficiently well to be placed in employment, although this is only done when the trainee has been able to hold down a job for at least six months of his training period. When this has been successfully achieved he is placed on the Disabled Persons Register and so, when he returns home from Slough, he comes under the care of the Disablement Resettlement Officer.

MB is a typical case. He was fifteen years eleven months old when he went to Slough, but his mental age was assessed at six years ten months, which gave him a functioning IQ of 48. Socially he functioned at the level of 8·6 years. Shortly before he was admitted his father died, and this produced some signs of behaviour difficulty. He was a highly nervous boy, whose problems were exacerbated by very bad facial acne of which he was acutely conscious. In spite of all these difficulties, with the help he was given he settled down in the community and became adjusted to hostel life. He made such good progress in the workshop and Centre that he was able to go out to work in a local industrial concern. To get there from the hostel he had to make a bus journey which involved two changes and this he learned to do successfully. When the time came for him to leave he was found a job as porter and house man in a residential hostel which was 150 miles from his home (there was no suitable job available in his home district). He settled in well and his employers are very satisfied with him. He copes satisfactorily with a train journey which involves two changes when he goes home for Christmas and other holidays.

This is a case of maximum success but it would be quite wrong to give the impression that it could always be expected if every severely handicapped child was given this sort of care and training. Success must also be measured in other terms. RE is a case in point. He was twenty-three when he went to Slough. He had a mental age of four years six months and a social age af six years. He was sent for a limited period by his local authority, since his mother had been finding him increasingly difficult to manage at home, although she is intelligent and deeply concerned. She realized that some of her difficulties were the consequence of her over-protectiveness, but found it hard to alter in this respect.

R. was not able to go to work, but he did benefit greatly from the experience of living in a community where he took part in group activities and learned to do simple household chores and to co-operate in living with other young people. His parents not only benefited from the rest, but they also realized the importance of following up the improved habits which R. had achieved and this they have successfully done.

Both cases illustrate different aspects of what can be achieved with appropriate care and training in a structured, positively orientated community. The Slough Centre has now been handed over to the local authority by the National Society for Mentally Handicapped Children, and many other local authorities are attempting to make similar provisions in their own areas. Each successful trainee who leaves them is a living demonstration of what can be done if a child, with the handicap of severe subnormality, is given proper care, training and understanding. It can be done – it is for us to choose which way of life we will provide for these children.

Conclusion

In this and the preceding chapters an attempt has been made to explain the nature and causes of subnormality and also to examine the provisions which are made for the care and education of children with this handicap. It is undoubtedly true that much progress has been made and it is also true that it would be totally wrong to single out for criticism any of the people or institutions who are attempting to provide the necessary services, often against great odds and with inadequate staff and resources. Nevertheless, there is clear evidence that we have little room for complacency, for there are grave defects and deficiencies to be found in every aspect of the care which we, the community provide for these handicapped members.

The parents of these children are equally handicapped with their child, and this extends to all the members of the immediate family. Only too often lack of proper co-ordination of the various social services involved results in the family being left unsupported in their time of greatest need, that is, in the period immediately after the child's birth. Frequently the parents are not told in acceptable ways the truth about their own child nor do they easily obtain advice or genetic counselling. If they decide to care for the baby at home the sad anomaly arises that the more competent they appear to be in coping with the problems of the situation, the more they are left to do so alone. It is also true that the whole family suffers economically from this decision. If, however, they decide on residential care, unless they are wealthy the majority have to accept that the community only provides hospital placement with all the deficiencies of this service that have been discussed. Even this provision is so inadequate that it is customary for each hospital to have waiting lists for beds so the whole family has to continue to live in conditions of stress and distress until a bed becomes available for the handicapped child.

Too many children are still admitted to mental hospitals purely because there is no other provision available to them. The mental health services as a whole have to function with financial resources which compare unfavourably with every other form of medicine. The amount of money allocated to research in this field is grossly inadequate although, as has been shown, research is urgently needed into every aspect of the problem.

Only now are detailed and careful investigations being carried out to plan the best means of improving the efficiency of the old training centres. However they are now the responsibility of the correct authority, that is the Department of Education and Science and there is hope that in a few years all the people working in them will have proper professional training and qualifications. The fact that these new schools are not set apart from the Schools for Slow Learners should lead both to their greater acceptance and also to flexibility of transfer of children as found to be appropriate.

The community as a whole is becoming more tolerant and accepting of the handicapped, although there are still all too frequent cases where neighbourhoods demonstrate that they prefer these children to be removed from their immediate neighbourhood. This rejection is also sometimes shown in personally hurtful ways as, for instance, when the mother of a handicapped boy was told by a neighbour, who was in many ways kind and friendly not to let her defective boy touch her son's toys. 'As if', said the mother, 'my little boy could taint them with his touch.'

It would be idle to pretend that there are still not many defects, it would be wrong and misleading to pretend that because the necessary legislation has been passed everything needed to bring the services to the desired standard will be available immediately. It will be many years before all teachers are trained teachers, before there are enough places in schools for all the children who need them, before all the schools are rehoused in buildings which are of the required standard, before enough hostels are built to prevent any child who does not need medical care being admitted to a hospital because there is nowhere else for them to go. This even if all the finance necessary is made available and it is still far from certain that this will be the case. The present mood of urgency must be sustained, the danger is that the public conscience will be satisfied by the measures being passed and it will not be known that they are still far from practical realization. Nevertheless the three fundamental changes brought about in 1971, i.e. the transfer of educational responsibility for all children from the Department of Health and Social Security to the Department of Education and Science, the establishment of local authority social security departments to take over the functions affecting the mentally handicapped (previously the province of the local health departments) and the publication of the Government White Paper with its detailed planning for improving and reforming the services for the Mentally Handicapped, do mark the establishment of a new era and one which must change for the better the lives of the mentally handicapped.

Part Three
Slow Learners

'Educationally subnormal pupils, that is to say, pupils who, by reason of limited ability or other conditions resulting in educational retardation, require some specialized form of education wholly or partly in substitution for the education normally given in ordinary schools.' (Category 2: Handicapped Pupils and School Health Regulations, 1945, defined by Minister of Education, following the Education Act of 1944.) This definition of educationally subnormal is significant for it displays two important changes in official thinking. In the first place the definition is not based, as in all previous Acts, on a clinical concept of 'mental deficiency' but on educational needs. Secondly, the category has been made very broad: it includes all children who are seriously backward and not just those who are of limited mental ability. An important consequence of this widened concept is that it has been officially recognized that it is impossible to draw a rigid line between children who are normal and children who are 'defective'. In other words, educationally subnormal children are now regarded as children who require special education suitable for their 'age, ability and aptitude'.

This category has now been enlarged still further since it now includes all the children previously found to be 'unsuitable for education at school'. The consequence is that 'slow learners' is now by far the biggest of all the groups of children considered to be in need of special education.

Over twenty years have gone by since this definition was published. In the following chapter, events leading up to the Education Act of 1944 are described and the changes brought about by its application are considered.

Chapter Five
Special Education

The growth of special education

The separate education of slow-learning children officially began with the passing of the Elementary Education (Defective and Epileptic Children) Act in 1899. Before the introduction of the universal system of compulsory education in this country by the Education Act of 1880, popular education had been provided by two voluntary agencies: the British and Foreign School Society and the National Society. They were unable to provide education for all children and, therefore, had to select from the applicants. Since the teachers worked under very stringent conditions and their salaries depended upon the children's ability to reach arbitrarily imposed educational standards – 'payment by results' – it was inevitable that priority of placement was given to the children who had some chance of reaching those standards. In consequence, very few dull children were admitted to these schools. The Education Act of 1870 required locally elected school boards to provide education for all who wanted it, and it soon became apparent that many children were not able to reach the standards set by the board; since there were frequently sixty or more children in one class, the wonder is, perhaps, that any did. The number of failures rapidly increased when education became compulsory after 1880, and it was chiefly because of the growing awareness of the problem, helped by the pressure exerted by the teachers and doctors, that the Act of 1899 was passed.

The positive advantage of this Act was that it gave statutory recognition for the first time to the need to make special educational provision for those children who could not benefit from that provided in the normal schools. Nevertheless, it divided children into two apparently clear-cut categories – those who were mentally defective and those who were not. The use of the term 'defective' gave rise to much prejudice against special schools, causing untold distress to many parents and to the children. In fact it would be quite unrealistic to pretend that this prejudice has now totally disappeared; I can remember two years ago being directed by a casual passer-by to the 'soppy school'. Also, I have been told by parents that they couldn't let their child play with the boys who lived nearby since they regularly taunted him because he went, not to the local primary school, but to the special school.

The Act of 1899 empowered local authorities to set up special schools and classes, and by 1900 several such classes had been opened, the first in Leicester. A subsequent Act, the Elementary Education (Defective and Epileptic Children) Act, 1914, extended the responsibility of the local education authorities by imposing on them the duty of making suitable provision for mentally defective children over the age of seven in their area. This duty was further extended by the Education Act of 1921 which stated (p. 3) that:

A local authority shall, with the approval of the Board of Education, make arrangements for ascertaining ... what children in their area, not being imbecile and not being merely dull and backward, are defective, that is to say, what children by reason of mental or physical defect are incapable of receiving proper benefit from the instruction in the ordinary public elementary schools, but are not incapable by reason of that defect of receiving instruction in such special schools and classes as under this part of this Act may be provided for defective children.

This Act again implied that these children were fundamentally different from normal children by the use of the descriptive term 'defective'. A comparison of *this* description with that used in the Regulations of 1944 quoted earlier shows immediately how great a change took place in the fundamental approach and official attitude to the problem in the twenty-three years between the two Acts. In the earlier, a clear-cut separation between the 'defective' and 'merely dull and backward' is believed to be possible and desirable; in the latter the recognition of an infinitely finely graded continuum and multiplicity of causes is implicit. In the earlier Act it is taken for granted that all such children must be removed from the ordinary schools; in the later Act this is not so for it speaks of 'education wholly or partly in substitution for the education given in ordinary schools'.

Between 1899 and 1922, 198 special schools came into existence. It might have been expected that, after the Act of 1921, which required education authorities to seek out and ascertain 'defective' children, many more such schools would have been set up, but by 1938 the number had been reduced to 154. Nevertheless, these schools were catering for a slightly larger number of children, some of them having been formed by the amalgamation of earlier schools. Needless to say, all material advances came to a standstill with the outbreak of the Second World War, and remained so until the Education Act of 1944 and the subsequent framing of the new regulations.

The development of the IQ test

This period, from 1899 to 1944, saw not only the beginning of 'special education' but was also the time when great developments took place in the field of psychology and the study of child development and the findings of both began to be applied to education. It was in 1905 that Charles Binet devised and standardized the first simple mental test as a reliable means for selecting the children who most needed special schooling in Paris. From this developed the whole field of standardized mental tests and the concept of the intelligence quotient, or the IQ as it is commonly known.

An IQ is obtained very simply. Initially, in constructing a test, the psychologist devises a whole series of questions and operations which he thinks should be within the capacity of a normal child at each stage of his development. These tests are then standardized by being given to a very great number of unselected children of each age to be measured. Those that the average number of children of each age can pass are regarded as being normal for that age, those that the majority fail are too difficult, those that the majority pass are too easy. Therefore a child who consistently passes all the tests for older children is above average for his age, while one who can only pass those for younger children is below average. The child who passes all the tests for his age but none above or below would be regarded as completely normal, and would have an IQ of 100. In fact this exact performance never occurs; slight variations of performance on the different items of the test above and below cancel each other out.

The intelligence quotient is the mental age as a percentage of the chronological age. The mental age is calculated as in the following example. A six-year-old child is given a battery of tests for the five-year-old age level and passes them all. The procedure is repeated using the tests for the six-year-old age level. Again the child passes them all. He is then tested on tests for the seven-year-old age level and passes three-quarters of these; on tests for the eight-year-old age level he passes a quarter, and fails all for the nine-year-old. His mental age is calculated by starting from the highest age level at which he passed all tests (in this case the six-year-old age level) and adding on a proportion of a year equivalent to the subsequent proportion of tests passed at each age level.

Table 1

| Age level of test | Proportion of tests passed | Mental age | |
		years	months
5	All	–	–
6	All	+6	–
7	$\frac{3}{4}$		+9
8	$\frac{1}{4}$		+3
9	0	–	–

Mental age = 7 years

(IQ = mental age × 100 ÷ chronological age = 7 × 100 ÷ 6 = 116.) Therefore, the mental age of the child in this example is seven years, which would give an IQ of 116. (If the child has failed any of the tests at the five-year-old age level, he would have then been given the tests for the four-year-old age level, and so on until he passed all tests for a particular age range. In the lower age ranges the tests are very unreliable.)

This objective technique of measurement is extremely useful and the scores obtained from it are still one of the chief ways of determining the correct educational placement for a child.

In 1946, the Ministry of Education made the following recommendation:

Past experience suggests that children cannot be educated at school when their intelligence quotient is below about 55. A slightly lower figure may be used in the case of younger children (50–55) and a slightly higher (55–60) for those approaching the end of their school life. [These children are held to be 'unsuitable for education at school'.]

The children for whom the day special school is the most suitable are to be found among those whose limited ability corresponds with an intelligence quotient of about 55 to 70 or 75. Those with lower intelligence (55 to 60 or 65 intelligence quotient) might all attend, but among those in the group with the higher intelligence more and more other factors have to be taken into account before a decision is made to send a child to a special school. ... There may be a small proportion of children with intelligence quotients over 70 who should be sent there if the local education authority thinks there are strong indications that this is the right course, but a child with an intelligence quotient over 75 should rarely find his way there as his recuperative powers are so much greater than those of the majority of the pupils in special schools that he would usually be out of place, and would be better in a class in an ordinary school in which special educational treatment is provided.[1]

This is still held to be valid but, whereas at one time the intelligence quotient was considered to be a fixed measure of a person's innate ability or intelligence, it is now much more correctly considered as a measure of that person's level of functioning at the time when the test is administered and in the areas which it measures. It is often said nowadays that more useful information for planning a child's education can be gained from studying his failures on such a test rather than his successes. It is also generally recognized that a child's performance on these tests is only a measure of one part of his behaviour and that many other factors need to be taken into consideration, such as his social and emotional development. (These factors are considered in the discussion of ascertainment later in this chapter.)

Nevertheless, the importance of Binet's original work cannot be overemphasized. Revisions of his original tests are still in constant use, and the subsequent development of mental testing played a big part in facilitating the study of individual differences and their implications in planning remedial treatment. The studies of Jean Piaget, Arnold Gesell, Susan Isaacs and many others, into child development, all of which were taking place in this period, led to further important advances in educational theory and methods. In 1913 the London County Council appointed Cyril Burt to be the first psychologist to advise a local education authority. The value of his work and its application to all aspects of special education is recognized by everyone in the field; not only are his own researches into the extent and causes of backwardness and delinquency of fundamental importance, but it is also true to say that the whole development of the school psychological service stems directly from his pioneer achievements. The years from the beginning of special education until the end of the Second World War were years of both achievement and consolidation; the local authorities began to accept and meet the need for providing special educational facilities; the growth of psychological knowledge and techniques led to greater understanding of the widely varying needs of children and indicated possible ways of supplying them.

The present position

The years since the passing of the 1944 Act have been years of change and expansion in all aspects. In January 1963, 37,000 boys and girls were being educated in special schools for slow learners, in addition many more were being helped in various types of special classes and centres. By January 1970 the totals had risen sharply. Table 31 (32) titled 'Educational provision for handicapped pupils' in *Statistics of Education* (1970) [2] gives the following figures for Educationally Subnormal children.

Table 2

Assessment and placement during 1969	Totals
Pupils newly assessed as requiring special educational treatment	12,271
Pupils newly placed in special schools or boarding	12,100
Reported as unsuitable for education in school under Section 57 (4) of the Education Act 1944	1336

Table 3

January 1970 *Pupils attending special schools*	*Totals*
Maintained day	44,540
boarding	7622
Non-maintained day	251
boarding	1280
Boarded in homes	17
Attending independent schools under arrangements made by Authorities	600
Receiving education otherwise than at school i.e. home tuition, tuition in hospitals, tuition in special classes and units not forming part of a special school	383
Total	54,693

A surprising fact which emerges from the records is that every year since 1949 the number of children who need but are waiting for placement in special schools has remained fairly constant at around 10,000. January 1970 was no exception for in the same table we find these figures:

Table 4

January 1970 *Awaiting admission to special schools*	*Totals*
(figures include some pupils attending ordinary schools or receiving home tuition)	
Day pupils	
Age 5 and over	8443
Under 5	68
Boarding pupils	
Age 5 and over	1971
Under 5	4
Total	10,486

The appalling fact also emerges from the tables that of the total above 4691 children had been awaiting suitable placement for more than a year.

It is extremely difficult to obtain accurate figures both of the number of children who require special provision and of those who are receiving it in one form or another. However it is generally held that at least 10 per cent of all schoolchildren are slow learners to some degree and require special educational treatment. Of these about 1 per cent go to special schools, the rest, in theory, are being provided for in the normal schools. Until fairly recently there was no systematic or accurate assessment of what and how this was being provided. During 1967–8 however a survey was carried out by HM Inspectors in Secondary Schools in various parts of England and the findings published in 1971. (Slow Learners in Secondary Schools Education Survey 15, HMSO 1971.) Some aspects of the quality of the help found to be provided in this way will be discussed later in the next chapter. The interesting fact at this point was that of a total population of 91,527 children in the schools surveyed 12,807 were considered by the head teachers in need of some measure of special education mainly as slow learners but only 54 per cent of these (6892) were actually receiving it in their present schools. There was a wide variation from school to school in the estimated number of children in need, overall it was 14 per cent, one school in seven claimed to have over 20 per cent. In one school the total was 60 per cent and the report states that in the special circumstances of this school this figure was not unrealistic. Over one-third of the head teachers considered they were providing adequately for the children but approximately one-tenth of the schools made no provision at all. Even if full allowance is made for the fact that secondary education was in the process of being reorganized in many areas it is clear that the position was far from satisfactory. It would be most useful if a similar survey could be carried out for primary and middle schools where they exist.

It should not necessarily be assumed from these figures that educational retardation is on the increase, more probably the larger totals are the result of other factors such as the greater willingness of head teachers to bring children forward for assessment and the growth of advisory facilities especially the school psychological services.

Resources allotted to special education

In January 1965, 4600 children of the 10,000 waiting for admission to the special schools for slow learners had been waiting for over a year, five years later in January 1970 there is a remarkable consistency in these figures as the tables given above show. Even these figures do not give a full picture of the inadequacy of the present provision. All of the most recent surveys such as the Isle of Wight Survey, the National Child Development Study and the DES Education Survey 15 referred to indicate that the percentage of children in need of special education is far higher in both primary and secondary schools than has previously been estimated. The proportion expressed as a percentage is approximately 14 per cent of the total. Some authorities make far more generous provision than others, for there is a wide variation as between one authority and another. Direct comparisons of the amounts spent by the different authorities on special education only gives a very rough indication of what is in fact being done as it takes no account of such things as incidence, alternative provision in normal schools, nor the sizes of the classes in the special schools. Nevertheless, it is interesting to note that according to *Education Statistics* (published by the Institute of Municipal Treasurers and Accountants), Liverpool, for example, spent £1353 per 1000 population in 1965-6 and this was more than six times the amount spent by Stockport. There is also a wide variation in the amount spent by the counties, ranging from £755 per 1000 population in Lincolnshire to £306 per 1000 population in Cornwall.

Another interesting estimate of the variation from one region to another can be found in the Report of the Chief Medical Officer of the Department of Education and Science which sets out the regional rates of ascertainment for handicapped children. These figures relate to children who have been ascertained as definitely needing special education in special schools. They reveal some fascinating material for further investigation since they show, but do not attempt to account for, the wide variation of ascertainment in the different regions of every kind of handicap – even of such acute physical conditions as deafness. As far as the slow learners are concerned the national average is 74·6 per 10,000 school population, but the regional range was from 49·9 to 92·1 per 10,000. The figures from all sources tend to reveal that the larger county boroughs spend most on special education. In January 1970 over 65,000 children in all were being given special education in special schools but unfortunately it was still only too true that one of the main determining factors to whether a child was so placed was purely where he happened to live.

Ascertainment procedures

An examination of the way in which children are identified and ascertained shows that there is also a wide variation in the procedures used and in the efficiency of such procedures. Ascertainment procedures should be aimed at finding out which children need special education and how and where it should be provided. Clearly this is not a simple matter. Under all the earlier Acts the duties of ascertainment rested solely with either the local medical officer or the assistant school medical officer. He would examine a child and then certify him as being 'mentally defective' and unable to benefit from education in the normal school. These certifying procedures, under the famous (or notorious) Section 55 of the Education Act, 1921, lasted until the framing of the new regulations in 1945.

Since the consequences of certification affected the whole future education and, hence, life of a child, one would have expected the medical officer to have been specially trained for the task. In fact he had no training at all until the NAMH initiated in 1920 a week's training course which the doctors attended on a voluntary basis only. It was not until 1937 that the course was extended to three weeks and made obligatory. There is no reason to doubt the medical competence of these doctors; it is extremely unlikely, however, that one would be prepared to put decisions relating to one's life and future into the hands of a person, who, however competent in other ways, had only three weeks' training for this particular task. Nevertheless, the future of many children has been, and still is, determined in this way in many parts of the country.

Since the passing of the 1944 Act, it is no longer necessary for this formal legal procedure to be followed although provision for it is still retained in Section 34 of the Act. Provided the parents of a child give consent there is no longer any statutory obligation for a formal decision to be taken by the local education authority prior to a child's admission to a special school. This informal procedure has many advantages, not the least of which is that it facilitates the transfer of a child in either direction. However, it does mean that there is an even greater need to use good ascertainment procedures.

Ascertainment can take place at any age, although it is obvious that only the most severely backward children will be identified in their earliest years. Normally the health visitor or family doctor makes the first report in such a case. The child is then seen at his home by the medical officer who examines him physically to see if there is any obvious reason for his retardation. The medical officer may discuss the child's social and developmental history with the parents to supplement the information given by the health visitor. He then administers a short version of an intelligence or performance test based on the original Binet tests. Frequently, ascertainment consists solely of the above procedure. An IQ is arrived at and if it is less than 50 the child is judged to be unsuitable for education in school. Between IQs 50 to 70, he may be admitted on trial to an infant's school or, if he is lucky and lives in a progressive area, he may be admitted to a special diagnostic unit of a nursery type.

These units are an excellent idea; although there is agreement on the desirability of an early recognition and assessment of the retarded child, at this early age it is very difficult to assess either the child's true mental ability or to what degree other factors are influencing his level of functioning. This is particularly true of children who live in an unstimulating environment or who come from a grossly inadequate or socially deprived home. Except in cases of clear subnormality, attendance at one of these centres should be a necessary preliminary stage before any decision is made as to the correct educational placement of slow-learning children up to the age of seven. They should, therefore, be part of the educational provision of every local education authority. Whether they would be better located as part of a training school, in a school for slow learners, in an ordinary infant school or in a 'day nursery' is debatable. I have seen excellent material provision made for them in all these settings. The most physically attractive were in two modern purpose-built training schools, and excellent work was being carried out in them.

Ascertainment does not take place for the majority of children until after they have gone to school. It is rarely necessary in the infant school, although, if the diagnostic units described above were available in every locality, more children could well be moved into them from the infant school. This would prevent the kind of situation I saw when visiting a junior training school. Three children – twin girls and a boy – had been admitted from the local infant schools. All three had IQs of between 67 and 80 but were so socially and emotionally immature that they could not be retained in the large classes of the infant schools. No one was happy about this placement, nor was it likely to effect an all-round improvement in the children's behaviour. Any social gains they achieved were likely to be counterbalanced by lack of the appropriate intellectual stimulus. Their level of intellectual performance had probably already been adversely affected by their immaturity which appeared to be due in part at least to poor housing and mothers unable to cope with several small children. Thus, the children who, with correct placement, might have functioned on an average level, were in danger of becoming more retarded. It had been 'Hobson's choice' to admit them to the training school since the local school for slow learners had no facilities for admitting children under the age of seven. Smaller classes in the infant school or earlier attendance at a nursery school, had one been available, might also have prevented this outcome. Unfortunately, this kind of placement may even be increasing as training schools are improving physically and are therefore more acceptable to the parents.

It is usually in the primary school that children who require special educational treatment can be properly selected; the majority of schools for slow learners admit children from the age of seven. From every point of view the sooner this selection takes place the better. At present, although the actual age of admission varies considerably from area to area, the average age is approximately ten years, and some children still are not admitted until they are aged from thirteen to fourteen. Not only does this mean that the task of the special school becomes more difficult the older the child is on admission, but it also means that precious years have been wasted for the child. A psychological problem is therefore frequently imposed upon the initial problem, for the child's consistent experience of failure can lead to all sorts of behaviour problems, and his failure to learn is exacerbated by his lack of special teaching.

Some advanced authorities have evolved techniques for preventing or minimizing late ascertainment. Some test all the children towards the end of their first year in the primary school, others in their last year in the infant school. Those children who appear to be falling behind are then investigated individually, and the necessary remedial measures are initiated. The majority of local authorities, however, still rely upon the teachers to bring forward for assessment those children whom they believe to need it. This not only puts a great responsibility upon the teacher, who is already coping with the large classes commonly found in the normal school, but is liable to be inadequate for many other reasons. These would include all the dangers inherent in subjective assessments, perhaps arising from personality clashes between teacher and pupils, in addition to such factors as staff changes or the child moving fairly frequently from one school to another. Some form of screening process at regular intervals would clearly be more efficient, although this process should always include the detailed knowledge which the teacher alone possesses about the children in her care.

The normal sequence of ascertainment is that the teacher and head teacher of a school first discuss the progress of the children. When a child continues to fail after the usual remedial resources at the school have been tried, the head teacher reports to the local chief education officer that special arrangements may need to be made, and approaches either the school medical officer or, if one is available, the educational psychologist (or both) for advice. At the same time, the parents should be seen (and, in fact, usually are) by the head teacher and fully informed of the steps that are being taken to help their child.

This procedure is universal up to this stage; from this point, however, there is great variation according to the provisions made by the differing local authorities. It is their duty and responsibility to decide on the basis of the reports which they have received what, if any, special provisions need to be made. Many local education authorities still delegate all the responsibility for investigating the child to the school medical officer who carries out the procedures previously described. In the opinion of nearly all experts in the field it is now thought that the rather superficial and personal assessment of social, emotional and intellectual development plus physical integrity which the standard form allows for is inadequate when a decision of such importance is to be made. They therefore recommend that ascertainment procedures should be much more comprehensive and carried out by a team of specialists which, at the very least, should include the teacher, the doctor and the psychologist, and that equal weight should be given to all their views. The findings of specialist investigation of any suspected contributory causes should also be at the disposal of such a team. An interesting suggestion is made in the report *Educating our Handicapped Children*,[3] which says: 'If assessments were done at regional centres by staff responsible to the DES it would ensure diagnosis by well-trained and experienced people, of whom there are not enough to be employed by individual authorities' (p. 8). This report goes on to comment: 'This would also tend to eliminate any question of local bias and in particular the effects of local variation in provision.' This latter point is important because unfortunately it is still true that where the local provision is poor, head teachers are failing to bring children to the attention of the authorities because they have learned by bitter experience that 'nothing ever happens' when they do so.

One further point should be made about these procedures: diagnosis and assessment should always be continuing processes, subject to periodic review. Whatever form they take, these procedures are always aimed at finding out which children are failing to learn. We now know that, although this failure is the distinguishing feature of the group, the group itself is in no way a homogeneous one, nor is there commonly one simple early-recognizable reason for each child's failure. The Ministry pamphlet [1] states categorically that 'Educational retardation may be caused by "limited ability" or by "other conditions" or, it may be, by both operating simultaneously' (p. 17). It also lists some of the other conditions which are commonly found. Included in these are such factors as poor school attendance for a variety of reasons, frequent changes of school, disharmony between home and school, psychological maladjustment and unsatisfactory school conditions such as over-large classes and unsuitable teaching techniques.

In this particular pamphlet it is interesting to note the very positive way in which statements are made, e.g. 'it is a matter of general agreement that intelligence cannot be substantially improved by any methods known to us at present' (p. 18). It emphasizes the innate basis of general intelligence. The changes of opinion brought about by the last fifteen to twenty years of research are vividly demonstrated by the statements in a later publication of the DES, *Slow Learners at School*,[4] which are altogether much less categoric and positive: for example, 'the various influences combining to form the child's environment exercise a wider and more potent effect on his devolpment than had once been assumed' (p. 7) and 'some children do in fact show significant increases in intelligence test scores as the result of special education' (p. 9). The general discussion of why children fail to learn is considerably more subtle and comprehensive in this pamphlet and much greater emphasis is placed on the varying possible reasons why latent abilities may remain unrealized – reasons which include emotional and physical deprivation, lack of stimulus and opportunity to acquire skills at the 'critical development' period and, importantly, inadequate language development. Although it is still accepted that a distinction can be made in the terms of basic potential, it also specifically states that 'children are not easily classified and an over-emphasis on any single characteristic such as IQ or attainment age may result in problems being over-simplified and categories being defined too rigidly' (p. 10).

Some slow-learning children

The statement that a child is backward or slow-learning in fact tells you very little indeed about him, nor does it make him a special type of child. Slow-learning children will differ from one another in personality, in background, in hobbies and interests and so on, just as all children differ from one another. A close study of the different possible reasons for their backwardness is essential if they are to be properly placed to meet their special needs. The following examples from my own experience will illustrate how complex an apparently simple problem can be. All the children concerned were failing to read competently at the age of eight. They were all living at home with their own parents and most had been retained with varying degrees of difficulty in the normal schools.

Donald was an only child with concerned middle-aged parents. Their home was spotless and the child always looked freshly scrubbed, even at the end of a day. He had a speech impediment and preferred to play at an infantile level and with much younger children. Even after individual help and a period in a day centre for maladjusted children his IQ was never higher than 67; his span of attention was limited to two to five minutes and his general level of achievement in every subject was retarded by more than three years. There was a great deal of evidence that in his earlier days he had been over-protected and constricted and also that his parents had settled into a very fixed pattern of married life which his arrival was not allowed to interrupt. He was kept in a play-pen until he went to school at five. This kept 'the home properly tidy' and Donald away from any possible contact with 'dirt and germs'. It was very difficult to determine the true extent of his potential ability.

Joan was the elder of two children, basically a calm happy child whose achievements were more than two years below average. Her mother had been in a special school; her father had left the ordinary secondary modern school from a C-stream class. Both were pleasant hard-working people who had remained in the same jobs for years on end. The younger brother was very backward. Joan had begun to be conscious of the fact that in spite of all her hard work (and she did work hard), she wasn't doing as well as the other children in her class and she was beginning to show signs of anxiety and depression.

Ronald was a cheerful 'cockney sparrow' in constant hot water partly because his favourite exclamation in every situation was

'Balls!'. Going to school at all was a tedious necessity to be dodged whenever possible. He had several brothers of similar temperament. One elder brother was regarded as a 'bit funny' because he actually enjoyed school and liked to read. However, this was regarded as a harmless eccentricity by the rest of the family. Neither parent was worried about their children's education. They earned a good living with market stalls and knew the children could do the same, while the 'telly' and the picture papers supplied them with all the information they needed. Ronald could see no point at all in bothering to learn to read and had a ready answer to all queries designed to show him its usefulness. His general conclusion was that 'with eyes in his head, and a tongue to ask with' and a brother who could read for him if all else failed, he was well equipped to deal with every contingency.

The attitude of James' father was in complete contrast to that of Ronald's. He was a shoemaker with a small business of his own and had to work extremely long hours in order to provide for the family's needs. He was very conscious of the fact that he had had only a minimal education and had decided that this was the reason that he had not been more successful in his working life. The elder child in the family was a girl and although the father wanted her to do well in school he did not put any great pressure on her to do so. With James it was a different story. Almost from the day he started school his father expected him to start to learn to read. When he felt that the school wasn't taking it seriously enough he decided to take a hand in it himself. Since he always worked well into the evening, this meant that he got James up early in the morning so that he could give him an hour's reading practice before breakfast. The results were catastrophic. James became over-tired, sullen, very aggressive at school and quite impossible to teach. The less he succeeded the more anxious and determined his father became to make him read. The mother appreciated her husband's motives and to a certain extent shared his anxiety, particularly when the school began to complain about James's behaviour and backwardness. For some reason it didn't occur to her to tell the school about her husband's early teaching sessions with James and his extreme anxiety that the child should read. She did appreciate that life was 'becoming a nightmare' for them all but, feeling defensive both of her husband and James, began to put all the blame on the school for not teaching him to read properly in the first place.

Peter at eight had been excluded, for behaviour difficulties, from the primary school and sent by his parents to a private school which also constantly complained of his behaviour. His mother in turn was bitterly critical of the way in which the school was trying to control him. He was wildly over-active, a 'constant fidget', very volatile in his behaviour, but also prone to burst into tears and complain bitterly at the least provocation. Every time he leapt up in his seat, which he did constantly, he seemed to knock something over. All his work was 'untidy' and very retarded and he couldn't concentrate on doing anything for more than a few minutes at a time. Nevertheless, he was intensely interested in all that was happening in the world and had an excellent fund of general knowledge and a good vocabulary. In contrast to his behaviour when trying to do something, if he started to tell a story or discuss something, it was absolutely impossible to break in or to stop him until he had got to the very end. He was very conscious of the fact that he couldn't read or achieve in other ways and tried to cover up the fact. He was becoming quite adept in diverting the teacher's attention by such means as starting an interesting discussion or offering to help with some chore whenever he felt the time to read was approaching. Frequently he claimed to feel sick or to have a headache.

Terry had never been able to go to school. Physically he was perfect, but he did not use speech at all and appeared to be quite unresponsive both emotionally and to all external stimuli. But he showed extreme ingenuity in getting all his wants supplied and would occupy himself for long periods either doing complicated figures or building with Lego. Although he gave no appearance of listening to music at the time it was played, later he would sing accurately and apparently to himself quite a complicated melody.

Many other cases could be quoted but these few above do illustrate how varied the problems of children with the same educational difficulty can be. Obviously they did not all require the same kind of special education, although they were all educationally retarded. Of them all, Joan and her brother were the ones who were most probably retarded because of limited potential; Donald illustrates the fallacy of assuming that there is a clear-cut dichotomy between backwardness due to innate dullness and that due to other causes. James and Ronald in their different ways were reflecting the influences of their environment. Peter, who had had a very difficult birth, possibly had suffered slight organic damage and had a minimal cerebral lesion, whilst Terry was possibly psychotic. All of them were affected in other ways by their inability to profit from normal education.

The different forms of special education which are available to help children such as these and others who fail to learn in normal classes will be discussed in the next two chapters.

Chapter Six
Special Classes for Slow Learners

Types of special classes

The educational needs of slow-learning children are at present provided for in several ways, all within the educational system and under the control of the Department of Education and Science. By far the greatest proportion is, in theory at least, catered for by special classes normally held in the children's own schools and planned as an integral part of the school. In some parts of the country, however, area special classes are formed which are either attached to one particular school in the area or are accommodated in separate buildings. The children who are selected as most needing special help in all the schools in that area attend them either on a part-time or a full-time basis. Separate from these and designed to fulfil a different need are the remedial classes which have been set up by some local authorities. These classes or units are sometimes held within the framework of the normal schools and may cater either for the children with severe learning difficulties within that school or for all the children who have such problems within a group of neighbouring schools. Frequently, however, they are held in separate buildings such as a converted private house or a small school which is used exclusively as a centre for remedial teaching. At these centres the children, as in the area classes, attend either part-time or full-time according to their particular need.

These different forms of special classes are distinguished from the special schools in various ways. The children attending them remain members of the community of a normal school and so are enabled to take part in its social, recreational and communal activities. Administratively, therefore, except for some of the separate remedial centres, they come within the jurisdiction of the head of the normal school, and the teachers are members of the staff of that school. Between them these classes provide for

90 per cent of all the children who require some extra help because of their retardation. The remaining 10 per cent of the children are mainly catered for in special schools for slow learners, which can either be day or boarding schools, with the emphasis being placed on the provision of day school places. The proportion of children attending them is roughly three to every one in a boarding school. In some rural and sparsely populated areas there is a hostel attached to the day school to provide accommodation for the children who live too far to attend daily. Close contact is maintained with their homes and the children frequently go home for weekends. In addition to this, a small number of children are taught at home by a visiting teacher. The number of children attending a special class either in a special school or in one of the different classes is always smaller than that in the ordinary classes, the maximum number permitted by the regulations in any one class being twenty.

Selecting children for special classes

The decision as to which form of special education is most suitable for any particular child should be based on a correct and individual assessment of his needs and deficiencies. His functional IQ is, therefore, only one of the factors considered: the others should include his emotional maturity, his level of social adjustment, the rate of progress which he appears to be making, any factors in his background which may be contributory and also any possible physical handicap. In general it is still the practice to send to the special schools those children whose learning processes appear to be typical of those displayed by children of 'limited ability' and whose IQ as measured by a standard test falls within the range of 50 to 75. At either end of this range the other factors mentioned above are given more weight when deciding whether placement in a special school is best for any particular child. However, although it is generally accepted that the child's needs are the salient reason for deciding placement, it is in fact frequently determined by other causes, not least of which is what provision happens to be available at the time in that particular locality. This is directly affected by the provision made by the local authority.

Since the education of slow-learning children must take account not only of their educational needs but also of the various reasons why they have failed to learn in the normal school, it is useful to appreciate the ways in which their learning processes resemble each other's and those of normal children, and also in which ways they differ. Enough has already been said to show that there is great individual variation in the causes of backwardness. Nevertheless, it is possible to postulate some general statements which appear to apply to the learning processes of children who are backward because of their limited ability and which do not necessarily apply to those children who are educationally retarded for other reasons. It is therefore fairly important to decide as soon as possible whether the child who is failing to learn is showing these particular characteristics, for on this will rest to a large extent the decision as to the correct special educational placement to supply his needs.

The severely subnormal child is distinguished by the very slow rate of his intellectual and emotional development and his need to learn by practical experience and by very finely graded steps. Even with physical maturity he is unlikely to have progressed beyond Piaget's second stage of cognitive development (see p. 88). The child who is deemed to be 'educable but of limited ability' will show many of the same characteristics, but to a lesser degree, and will often progress to Piaget's third stage. He is in fact further along the continuum towards the mean. Nevertheless his development of language and vocabulary will proceed at a much slower pace than that of the other children of his age group and he will probably be backward in learning to read. His ability to form concepts and to generalize from experience will also be much slower both in development and in function, and he will need many more experiences before this process takes place. He will need much assistance to analyse and learn from every situation and much practical experience aimed at developing his powers of thought and understanding. However, the repetitions of each experience will need to be subtly different so that the child is kept continually interested and thinking. He will need to have his attention much more positively and continually directed to what is happening in the world around him. For example, whereas a child of normal ability may not even need to be shown that buses are numbered and that their number soon gives a quick indication of their route, the child of limited ability will need to have this fact first pointed out to him and then frequently repeated and demonstrated first for one bus, then for another until gradually he begins to understand the basic principle.

These are some of the most easily observed characteristics of the children with limited ability. They may also be shown in part by the children who are 'backward for other reasons'. For example, the child from a very deprived, unstimulating home may also have a very poor language development and appear to be lacking in the ability to learn from experience purely because he has had little opportunity to develop it. This possibility should be indicated by his history, however, and if this kind of child is given skilled help and teaching in a carefully designed and constantly stimulating environment, his rate of learning and maturation in general will prove eventually to be much faster than that of the child of limited ability. He will also prove to be more capable of meeting the social demands of the school community and of being able to join in such activities as sport, at a more equal level. The child of limited ability needs not necessarily be any slower at running about on a games field than any other child, even though he is more likely to suffer from minor physical handicaps, but he will lack the ability to sum up the changing situation rapidly enough to lead to anticipation of his best placement for the next move in the game. It is true, as many researchers have shown, that the higher the level of intellectual functioning a child has, the more likely he is to be superior in every other way. Unfortunately the converse is also true. The statement is often loosely made that the slow-learning child is 'good with his hands' and this can lead to the assumption that this means in comparison with the normally functioning child. In fact it means more accurately that his achievement in practically based work is higher than his own achievement in other ways.

There has recently been growing controversy as to whether all limited learning ability where there is no neurological or other physical damage is not the result of lack of the essential experiences at the correct maturational phase, rather than the consequence of an innate lack of intellectual ability. This is an interesting hypothesis which merits much detailed experimental research and which may ultimately radically alter many facets of our educational system, particularly of very young children. However, even if this supposition is eventually supported by evidence, it is reasonable to base our present special educational services both on the fact that this limited learning ability exists at present with some children whatever the prime cause of it eventually proves to be, and also on the knowledge which has been acquired so far as to the best milieu to supply the differing needs of the children affected.

Since it appears that the child who is backward because of limited ability needs the opportunity to learn at a slow rate and chiefly through frequently repeated practical experiences, and since his limited ability is likely to put him at a disadvantage in all the social and recreational facilities of a normal school, it is reasonable to think that his needs are better met in a special school. It is generally assumed that the needs of the child who is backward for other reasons are more likely to be satisfactorily met by the partial withdrawal provided by the different forms of special classes.

Special classes attached to normal schools

By far the greater number of special classes exist, in theory at least, as part of the routine organization of the normal schools. Their actual existence and the effectiveness of the provision they make, however, are very variable, and are affected by many changing factors. Usually the average size of the classes in normal schools is the maximum number permitted by the regulations. The situation is sometimes easier in this respect in the secondary schools than in the primary schools. In general, however, classes are too large to provide for the necessary care and attention to the individual needs of the pupils who most need it. Nor, partly for this same reason, is there usually adequate space and facilities for the type of active education which these children require. *Circular 11*, published in 1961 by the Ministry of Education, recommended that a room should be specially designed in all new schools and added to existing ones to meet the needs of the special class in each school. It was suggested that part of this room should resemble a workshop with sinks and mains services available and that from it there should be easy access to out-of-doors practical activities. Sheer economic factors have made this a dream rather than a reality for the majority of schools.

More important even than good premises is the quality of the teacher and the general attitude of the whole school, staff and children to the special class. There are still many schools which design the community and the curriculum to cater for the needs of the most able children in the school. In such schools it is these children who are taught by the most experienced teachers, while the less able tend to be put in the care of the youngest or most recently appointed member of the staff. The curriculum for the less able groups is also frequently based on a watered-down version of that designed for the most able. It should vary to meet the different needs of each group to enable them to develop and learn in the way most suited to them. This watering down is partly inevitable while there is an over-all insufficient supply of teachers: at present there is too little opportunity for teachers to do anything other than attempt to deal as competently as they can with the immediate situation. While schools are under-staffed nobody can expect that every child will get what is best for him. Often the most that can be achieved is to do as well as possible for the majority. In these conditions it frequently happens that any particular consideration will tend to be given to the children who soon demonstrate their ability to profit from the education provided, as they are the most rewarding.

Often the head of the normal school, who is responsible for designing the curriculum for the school, is usually much more knowledgeable about the needs of the normally functioning child. It is extremely unusual to find that he has special knowledge of the problems of the slow learner. This situation can be alleviated if there is a teacher on the staff with this specialist knowledge to whom the head can delegate the task of planning and supervising the work of the slow-learning children. This sometimes happens in the larger schools but rarely in the smaller ones, and is one reason why the problem of making special provision in the normal schools tends to be more acute in these smaller schools, which are usually more commonly found in the junior age group. It is particularly unfortunate, therefore, that this is the time that the slow-learning children really begin to need a specially designed curriculum for part of their work. They can happily continue to take part in much of the music, physical education and creative work of the rest of their age group, but their other work, especially reading and arithmetic, needs a different approach – one that is geared to give them the opportunity of succeeding. To help with this problem many head teachers arrange to free the class teacher so that she can give extra attention to those needing it, or they personally take small groups for reading practice in their own room. Sometimes, however, the other demands make it impossible for them to give this help regularly and this considerably reduces its value.

The most fortunate schools are those who can call upon the additional help of a peripatetic or part-time teacher, particularly if this visiting teacher is specially appointed because of her interest in this particular kind of work. This extra help is often one of the first things to be rescinded when an economic crisis arises. For example, in March 1968 this trend was already appearing. Some local education authorities were proposing not to take up their full quota of teachers, although it was recognized that this would lead to even larger classes. Others were economizing by cutting down on the number of part-time teachers. All the evidence indicates that the ultimate cost of such measures in terms of delinquency and malfunctioning is likely to be much greater financially, let alone in terms of human happiness, than the apparent immediate saving.

The greatest advantage of the larger schools, particularly the secondary ones, is that they can, because of their numbers, organize a series of classes for the more backward children and so form a special community within the larger community. When this is the case the responsibility for designing and organizing the work of these classes is more frequently given to one teacher who often has special training in the work. This arrangement gives children the opportunity to progress from one class to another but at the same time to be taught in a consistent manner. In theory this special community is not cut off from the larger group since the children will take part in the life of the school and will join with the other classes for the same kind of activities as do the backward children of junior age.

Between these two kinds of provision come the schools which are able to arrange one special class for all the backward children in that school. The success or failure of this arrangement is particularly vulnerable to the attitude of the whole school to its 'special class'. In a sympathetic school with a willing and experienced teacher, it can be a happy and stimulating environment giving security and stability to the children selected to form it. The disadvantages are that the age range within the class will be very wide and that the children may be at different levels of emotional maturity and physical and intellectual development. Also, since they may be in this class for some years, they will lack the stimulus afforded by the opportunity of progressing from one class to another. In an unsympathetic school it can lead to a hopeless situation, where a possibly inexperienced or unwilling teacher is faced with all the 'rejects' of the other classes. In either event there is no doubt that all the other children in the school are aware of the reason why the children are in this special class, no matter how it is named or described. I have heard them described in various ways by the other children – ways which ranged from the cruel, to the kindly but patronizing comment of a nine-year-old boy: 'Oh well, we don't expect much of them because that class is for the children who aren't quite with it.'

Until fairly recently there had been no surveys designed to estimate the efficiency of this kind of provision although there did appear to be some evidence that very good work was being done in some of the special classes in the normal schools. It was more a matter of faith than of established fact, that children in special classes in the ordinary schools did genuinely benefit from being members of this type of community. In 1963 the Ministry of Education (as it then was) published the results of a survey which set out to critically examine the consequences for some deaf children who after a period of special educational treatment were transferred to normal schools as they were judged to be able to make the transfer and likely to benefit from it.[1]

Although the findings are suggestive rather than conclusive, since the numbers involved were small, this report showed that in the cases examined the circumstances needed to be exceptionally favourable for the deaf child to make good academic progress in the normal school, and that even then it was likely to be less than what he could have been expected to achieve with his measured intellectual potential. What could not be objectively measured but appeared to be highly significant was the strain imposed upon the deaf child by his attempt to appear to be an integrated member of the community. Several examples of this are quoted and the statement is made that 'observation of all the children showed the great strain that they must endure in order to maintain their identities among people who are much better endowed than themselves and who hear well' (p. 28). Clearly a direct parallel cannot be drawn between the experiences of individual deaf children and groups of slow-learning children in normal schools, but it is at least possible that the statement quoted above, with the exception of the last four words which could be altered to 'and who comprehend well', when applied to the experiences of the slow learner, might be equally true.

In 1971 the Department of Education and Science published their Education Survey 15 already referred to in the previous chapter which did set out to investigate 'how successful ordinary schools were in providing for children with an apparent diversity of handicapping conditions' (introduction p. 5). The conclusion they came to indicated that there are many faults to be remedied if the service is to be effective. They found that when children classified as educationally subnormal were nevertheless placed in ordinary schools, some proved to achieve quite well but 'The pupils of least ability, however, were often observed to be needing a greater measure of skilled attention than they could be given and to be the odd men out in the secondary schools' (p. 4). One reason for this might well be that in half of the schools surveyed there were no 'fully satisfactory arrangements for the systematic identification of pupils' special needs' (p. 5) nor were the teachers well informed about the children's special needs when they transferred from the primary schools. In only one aspect did the survey find that things were 'satisfactory' and that was in the social life of the house units which were commonly set up in the schools. In all else things were far from satisfactory, the right equipment and facilities to cater for the needs of slow learners 'seemed to be given low priority' (p. 11) in many of the schools. Very few schools had special departments or had allotted graded posts to the teachers working with the children, a very low proportion of these teachers had had any specialist training or experience for the work, and in many instances since the children in the remedial departments (as they are commonly called) did not join the classes of specialist teachers there was even a less generous pupil–teacher ratio than for the more able children in the school. Although in most areas local courses of in-service training were available and reasonable opportunities were given to teachers to attend very few chose to do so.

In designing the curriculum where any attempt was even made to do this, there was the persistent and overall tendency to regard the work as a 'remedial' exercise and to concentrate attention on attempts to improve the basic skills. In consequence the statement is made 'limited achievements within a largely unsuitable curriculum are, therefore, characteristic of slow learners in many of the schools visited' (p. 17).

Although it is emphasized in the survey that since the schools were not mathematically selected no level of statistical significance can be attributed to its findings, it is also stressed that the schools were carefully selected to represent a true cross section, therefore results do 'provide a reasonably reliable picture'. Reliable and very disquieting, since it is quite obvious that the majority of children with special needs are not, at present, having proper provision made to meet their needs. The answer is not, and never will be, more special schools, since this is impracticable and totally unnecessary; it is to improve the facilities offered in the ordinary schools. First and most importantly, it appears to be necessary to educate the head teachers and other staff, to understand and appreciate the fact that these children do have special needs and that they must be allotted higher priority in equipment and resources. Secondly, in order to attract teachers of the right calibre and with the correct professional training and expertise, many more special departments within the schools will have to be set up and a much higher proportion of the posts within these departments will have to be upgraded in status and salary. When this has been achieved much else will follow, for such teachers will appreciate the need to analyse and identify the children's special needs, will understand the significance and importance of encouraging language development, of extending learning opportunities within and without the classroom and of designing a curriculum which is really educational in the widest possible sense. Thirdly, better and more efficient ways of obtaining and passing on relevant information will have to be developed.

Area special classes

When an area special class is accommodated within one school in that area, the comments and questions discussed above are equally applicable. If it is housed in a separate building it leads to further questions, the most important being what it is supposed to do for what type of child. Since the numbers attending it from each of the separate schools cannot be large, it cannot possibly be considered as a complete way of providing for all the children who need special help because it does not relieve the need of supplying it within their own school. If the answer is that it caters for the most severe cases, then it is difficult to understand why it is to be preferred to the much wider opportunities that placement in a special school would offer. On the other hand if it is meant for the children who may only need special help for a limited period, it would seem reasonable in all the circumstances to think that this help would be better supplied in their own school, where again the life as a whole would be much wider and more varied than a separate class for retarded children could hope to offer. It is possible that the main usefulness of the area classes is merely to provide a temporary solution in those areas where overcrowding and severe staff shortages made it impossible, at the time when the class was set up, even to consider providing special classes within the contributing schools.

Remedial classes

The remedial classes, designed to cater for a limited period for children who appear to have fallen behind for such reasons as frequent or prolonged absence, or frequent changes of school, or because of a personality clash with a particular teacher or school, are a totally different proposition and appear to be much more obviously logical and useful. The task of the teacher in these centres is not a simple one, since she has to design individual programmes for a group of children who are conscious of failure and who have come from different schools which possibly all use different teaching methods. Not only does she have to deal with the children's individual behavioural reaction to failure, but she somehow has to help them to adjust to each other sufficiently to allow the group as a whole to function. Moreover, since many of the children spend part of the time in their normal school, the work of the centre and each separate normal school needs to be co-ordinated, so as not to cause the child further problems by creating comparisons and arousing conflicting loyalties. Partly for these reasons there has been some controversy over the usefulness of remedial classes or centres. Once again there has been no co-ordinated, statistical assessment of their value. There is commonly, however, local knowledge as to the value of any particular centre; from this kind of information it appears that their success as measured by improved educational achievement and social adjustment is variable and that some children lose what they appeared to have gained after their return to the normal schools. This is yet another area where research is needed into every aspect of the subject.

Placement for some individual children

It might be interesting at this point to consider briefly the placements decided upon for the children whose cases were quoted in the previous chapter. Ronald, James and Donald were all recommended for part-time attendance in a special class which was not part of a normal school. Ronald began to get interested in attending this special class when he found that he could have a garden of his own in the grounds of the house in which the class was held. Once he had dug and planted it, he even popped into the garden regularly at weekends and throughout the official school holidays to tend to it. Through doing this he became interested in all the birds which he noticed and soon wanted to know their names and more about them. The teacher freely confessed her own ignorance but took Ronald to the local bookshop where they chose together a well-illustrated book about the identification of birds. Ronald soon became quite adept at finding a possible picture of the bird but had inevitably to rely upon the teacher to read the identifying data. Since by the time she was free the bird frequently had, literally, flown, she was able to point the moral that it would be much simpler if he learned to read the information for himself. This he finally decided to do and it was quite an epic day for all when, after he had begun to be some-what proficient, he suddenly announced, 'Reading makes sense!' Ultimately he did not need to attend the special class but for a while he did continue to call in to work at his garden. Finally the other outside interests of the normal school replaced this, par-ticularly after he moved up into the secondary school. He still was not a totally conforming orthodox boy, but the school was well able to contain him, the one complaint from the head teacher being that he found it difficult to keep the library suffi-ciently stocked to cope with his voracious reading!

James was a more difficult problem. Even after his father understood that he was to a certain extent defeating his own object, he could not stop attempting to drive the child towards his idea of what he should be achieving. Eventually James was helped to understand his father's motives and to appreciate that life would be happier for them all if, instead of resisting, he in fact worked to outstrip his father's standards. As he matured this became simpler for him to comprehend. The situation also became easier when for a while the father was unwell and had to stop all work, even his attempts to teach the boy. James also was successfully returned to the normal school after a fairly long period of attendance at the special class.

With both these children the class had been able to give the help which they needed. With Donald it was less successful. Even after a long period he remained an immature child who could not concentrate his attention on anything at all for longer than a few minutes. His slight speech defect persisted and he still pre-ferred to play in an infantile manner and with younger children. At the age of ten he could barely read, write or count. Although everyone concerned still felt unable to come to a firm conclusion as to his true intellectual capacity, it was nevertheless decided that he would be best helped by placement in a school for slow-learners, which would give him the advantages of being taught in a smaller class and with more practically based work. It would also mean that he would have an extra year in school and more special consideration when the time came for him to leave school and attempt to find work. Even at the end of this time in the special school, he still remained a largely unsolved problem and was only employable because he was fortunate enough to be taken on by a family friend and so could get the maximum support and tolerance both at home and at work. The ultimate prognosis is very uncertain.

For Terry the future was even less happy. He also attended a special unit for a while and showed many signs of greater awareness and responsiveness. However, this unit was chiefly designed for younger children and as Terry got older he began to have periods during which he became very noisy and aggressive, chiefly to himself. This became too frightening for the other children so he had to be kept at home. The parents coped for as long as they could, but eventually he became too violent for his mother to control him when he was in his aggressive moods. He is now a patient in a psychiatric hospital. This might possibly have been inevitable in any event, but on the other hand, everyone who knew him is now wondering whether he would have been improved had the special unit to which he was admitted at the late age of thirteen and a half, and in which he did begin to improve, been opened and available to him ten years earlier.

Joan, like Donald, was a case where the choice of special placement was difficult. She could possibly have obtained the help she needed in a special class but her brother was obviously going to need placement in a special school and the parents wished the children to attend the same school if possible. This by itself would not have been a sufficient reason for deciding in favour of a special school for Joan, but taken in conjunction with her own growing unhappiness at being unable to keep up with the children in the normal school no matter how hard she tried, it was decided that she and her brother should go to a day special school for slow-learners.

Investigation showed that Peter was a case where there was a definite minimal cerebral lesion and his further progress is discussed in chapter 10.

Conclusion

No matter where the special classes are held the facilities which they offer must be balanced against their varying disadvantages. The extent to which they exist in the normal schools is difficult to establish: even where the school is sympathetic, special classes are vulnerable and particularly susceptible to the effects of such factors as staff changes and shortages. All the most recent surveys show that there are many more children in the normal schools who need special help than has ever been appreciated. So far no evidence has been obtained as to how efficiently primary schools, and – where they exist – middle schools also, meet the needs of these children. The *Survey of the Slow Learners in Secondary Schools*[2] reveals that there are gross inadequacies and overall very little understanding and appreciation of what should be being attempted. There has been too little controlled observation and experimental research even into the work done in the special classes. Many of the individual classes do keep careful records of the children who attend them, and even their subsequent records when they have left, but these are not collated or analysed in the attempt to answer such questions as why one particular class really is more successful than another. Success could be due to different selection of cases, more skilful teaching, more social harmony within the group, better relationships with the parents and the contributing schools, or a combination of all these things, and the special skills of the teacher. A teacher's personality, in addition to her professional ability, might be crucial.

A great deal has been done in recent years to give special help and attention to the child who requires it. The need to make special provision has been accepted and embodied in the Education Act; the next step appears to be to examine critically the ways in which attempts are at present made to supply it and then give practical application to the results of the findings, which in due course should again be subject to critical reviews and possible redevelopment. Special education, in common with all other types of education, must be a growing, living, changing process constantly based upon the application of new knowledge and information of every aspect involved.

Chapter Seven
Special Schools for Slow Learners

The function of special schools

Special schools exist to provide education for those children who need more individual attention than can be provided in any of the different classes in normal schools. They are intended, therefore, to cater for the children at either end of the continuum – both the gifted and the handicapped – for it is perfectly valid to consider the grammar and other schools designed to provide for the needs of the gifted child, as 'special schools'.

The present situation with regard to slow-learning children is that approximately one in ten of those found to need special help are sent to special schools, which are either day or boarding schools. The number of these schools, especially day schools, is still increasing, for the greater emphasis has been and probably always will be placed on their provision. There is a clear need for this increase: in January 1965 approximately 10,000 children who had been ascertained as needing to attend such schools were awaiting placement, and 4600 of them had been waiting for over a year. These are minimum figures for, as was discussed earlier, they do not give any indication of the number of suitable children who, for one reason or another, have not been brought forward for ascertainment. The emphasis on the provision of day schools rather than boarding schools is soundly based on economical, social and humane considerations, for it is now commonly accepted that no child should be sent away to school unless there are over-riding reasons for doing so. The boarding school for slow-learners is designed for those children:

1. For whom it is administratively impossible to provide day school facilities since they come from rural areas where the population is scattered and transport is difficult to provide.

2. Whose home conditions are unfavourable, or which have totally broken down.

3. Who have severe behaviour disturbances in addition to their 'limited' ability.

In the spring 1966 issue of *Special Education*, Tansley reported on a survey of 100 slow-learning children who attended the Birmingham residential special school of which he was headmaster at the time.[1] This survey presented evidence that 75 per cent of these children were likely to have been at risk from a very early age because of possible damage to the central nervous system after the 'occurrence of unusual pre-, post- and peri-natal conditions and physical trauma in infancy' (p. 15). The percentage of disturbed home backgrounds was lower than expected.

Although the findings of this survey are tentative and limited by the difficulties of obtaining objective assessment, and although the sample of children was highly selective – the school caters for Birmingham children who are slow-learners and more or less seriously maladjusted – the evidence points to the need for close and early observation of all children who are known to be at risk. If the parents and teachers of these particular children had been alerted to the possibilities, they might have been able to prevent the development of such severe behaviour problems. Further research is needed to establish whether this trend is general, and to investigate preventive measures that could well, in time, reduce the incidence of children needing residential rather than day provision. This is just one example of the many subjects for research which exist in the whole field of special education – subjects which are not just esoteric, but which could have important practical applications.

Most of the larger urban areas have at least one day special school, and although some of them have been in existence for many years the majority have been opened since the last war. In consequence, a high proportion of them are modern in design, reasonably comprehensive in the provision of workroom facilities of one kind or another and attractive in their appearance. This has been a very useful factor as it has helped many an anxious and disappointed parent to accept the special school.

Educational aims

It is interesting to compare the stated aims on which the education of the slow-learner in these schools is based with those found by Simpson to be the basis of much of the teaching in the training centres (see chapter 4, p. 75). Even in a pamphlet, *The Education of Backward Children*, published as long ago as 1937 by the Board of Education, the following statement is made:

Expressed in broad general terms our aim in the education of dull children must be to enable them to lead a life of useful service to others and of happiness to themselves. In pursuit of this aim we shall have to inquire what useful habits should be inculcated, what forms of skill it is necessary they should have opportunities of acquiring, what types of knowledge they should assimilate and what interests and what attitudes of mind they should be led to develop (p. 30).

The terminology is somewhat old-fashioned, but the aim itself has much in common with that stated today. In *Slow Learners at School* [2] we read:

The aims of education for the backward are not fundamentally different from those for any other children – the fullest development of their personalities and talents within the society in which they live, so that they may grow into responsible and acceptable adults. The most successful schools have provided an education that recognizes each child's combination of abilities and limitations, conscious that purely intellectual achievements will almost certainly mean far less to him as an adult than a pleasing personality and a dependable character (p. 56).

Tansley and Gulliford in their sound and comprehensive account, *The Education of Slow-Learning Children*, [3] give a full account of their concept of the aims on which the education of these children should be based (p. 88). The whole is too long to quote here, but the two general aims are stated to be:

1. The development of personal adequacy, which involves the maintenance of physical and mental health, the eventual achievement of economic efficiency, the ability to use leisure time wisely and the acquisition of the necessary basic skills and habits.

2. The development of social adequacy. This involves training in forming social relationships and in the development of good citizenship.

In the same chapter, Tansley and Gulliford make an interesting distinction between the individualization of treatment and individual treatment. The first term describes the need to base a child's teaching programme on a careful study of his needs, the second the need to teach the child apart and on his own. The first is essential in any form of special education – the second should only be resorted to in very special circumstances since an essential part of the education of all children is the provision of continuous opportunities to learn to live and work as a member of a group.

This latter is, in one sense, the major aim of the residential schools, dealing as they do, in the main, with children who are disturbed in some form or other. Even the children who come to them from stable homes in rural areas, and who are not maladjusted, are nevertheless uprooted and frequently nervous and ill-prepared for facing life without the support of their family group and familiar surroundings. These schools are, therefore, usually small, or if they cater for large numbers they are normally subdivided to form smaller 'family' groups within the main group.

It is almost a truism that the success of any type of school depends upon the personal qualities of the head teacher and his staff. This applies particularly in such a boarding school since the staff must have insight into all the needs of the children plus the ability to live and work harmoniously in a specialized community which is not only a school but also a substitute home for disturbed and slow-learning children. The demands made upon them are great and this is frequently recognized by the local authority providing a higher staff ratio than is prescribed in the regulations. However, this is not invariably so and often even well-disposed authorities are unable to provide as many staff as they would wish, partly for financial reasons and partly because with present conditions of service and emoluments, both for the teaching and non-teaching staff, it is increasingly difficult in a competitive market to attract sufficient staff of the right calibre. For this reason far too many teaching staff are doing far too many hours of duty in the out-of-school periods, and for rather inadequate financial compensation. This is a destructive process since it is bound to lead to tension, over-fatigue and a general feeling of uneasiness which inevitably adversely affects the children. Nevertheless, the evidence shows that the good boarding schools are achieving real success with some of the most difficult children, many of whom experience for the first time in their lives complete physical care, good human relationships and a way of living and learning specially designed to cater for every facet of their lives and development.

The actual curriculum and school-work programme is not essentially different in the day and boarding schools. The whole trend of education in general has moved away from planning an educational programme in terms of the subjects to be taught to developing and supplying the child's needs and capacities. This is especially valid in the special schools; indeed the whole movement partly began in these schools where gifted teachers relaized that any watered-down version of the curriculum of the normal school was of little value.

Tansley and Gulliford suggest that the curriculum for these children should be

composed of two closely linked and interdependent parts:
1. A central core of language and number.
2. A periphery of additional useful knowledge about the environment, creative and aesthetic activities and practical interests.

In all special schools and classes for slow-learners the teaching of the basic skills is consistently related to practical experience and the development of language. Planned syllabuses of separate subjects such as history, geography, etc., are rarely if ever used in these schools. Instead, the children first explore and study their own locality and later make longer excursions to study a different one. Similarly, their scientific experiences are based on practical everyday life, such as observing and recording the weather, studying the development of plant and animal life by growing and caring for them, visiting gas, water and electricity works, and so on. In the later school years the emphasis is placed upon preparing the children for taking a full and active independent role in the community. In the earlier days of special education, attempts were made to teach a trade – to give direct vocational training; now the emphasis is on the development of sound attitudes to work, experience in handling tools and machines of all kinds, the achievement of self-discipline and the ability to assume responsibility for their own life and conduct. In other words, it is designed according to the primary needs of everyday living in the community.

One special school

Before considering some of the wider aspects of the present trends in special schools it might be interesting to describe briefly a typical school for slow-learners. It is purpose-designed and was opened in September 1960; it accommodates 120 children between the ages of seven and sixteen. The records show that there are consistently more boys than girls on the roll. The school, which stands in its own grounds, is on a main road on the outskirts of a reasonably large town and within easy access of buses, trains, shops, etc. There is a zoo nearby and many small factories and market gardens. It is the custom in this area for school uniforms to be worn and the children attending this school wear one similar in design to those of the other neighbourhood schools. The intelligence range of the children over the last three years was as follows: in 1965 from a postulated 36 to 95; in 1966 from 40 to 95; in 1967 from 46 to 95; with the maximum number in each year falling within the range 56 to 80.

The following cases are typical of the children at the extremes. At the lower end are two non-communicating, very withdrawn boys, both of whom are being referred for fuller investigation; one is suspected of being psychotic and the other of suffering from minimal cerebral palsy. Their measurable IQs are both under 50. At the higher end of the school's range there is a boy, IQ 91, with minimal cerebral palsy, which has resulted in slight ataxia (a loss of co-ordination of voluntary movements) and dyslexia (word blindness); another, with IQ 86, 'in care' to a local authority, was, on admission, both underfunctioning and severely maladjusted. Among the other children in the school are several who have minor physical disabilities, and two (boys again) who suffer from phenylketonuria which is being corrected by carefully controlled diet. They are kept under close and constant review and referred instantly to hospital when there is any significant change in their behaviour or level of functioning.

The headmaster, Mr D. J. R. Morrison, has drawn up a memorandum, a copy of which is given to each member of the staff on joining the school. In it he sets out the aims of the school and the principles which underlie his whole approach, and then goes on to discuss and consider the teaching of the various 'subjects'.

The following brief quotations will indicate the way in which this school functions.

Some of the principles and aims of our work are to equip these handicapped children:

to take their place in life;
to be able to take up suitable employment and be self-supporting;
to accept and overcome difficulties;
to give education up to their capacities;
to enable them to become emotionally stable;
to make them socially competent;
to develop through moral and spiritual training an appreciation of the good, true and beautiful.

This work will make great demands on the staff, not only in their application of teaching skills but also on their human qualities. They should possess sympathetic understanding, an unlimited patience and perseverance, a sense of humour, and not be easily frustrated. Results in this work are often exceedingly slow and one should not despair, for the eventual results usually compensate for these efforts.

Later he writes:

Most of the subjects taught in this school are considered from the point of view of acquiring skills through which our children can express themselves and so communicate with their environment, thus our subjects are regarded as varying forms of language. . . .

All subjects must have the flavour of authenticity for each child in so far as those parts of the curriculum presented to him at each stage of his development are connected with the world he knows to exist and part of which he has experienced.

These basic principles are then applied to the consideration of each 'subject' in turn, coupled with a brief discussion of the particular value of each in the context of the over-all aims. This is followed by practical advice and a list of the books and materials available in the school.

Equal care and thought has been put into providing for the social life of the children both in and out of school time: they play games against the normal schools, wherever this is possible, and have club evenings. The staff try to prepare them in the school for the demands of adult life, and then settle them into a job when the time comes for them to leave.

The following accounts are typical. Three boys, who left in 1965, went to work in nursery gardens. Two of them, with functioning IQs of 48 and 59, were working well with the foreman and earning about £5 9s. od. a week; the third, with a functioning IQ of 78 and a reading age of 8 years 4 months, was not only working well but had also been accepted for a one-year training course in gardening at a 'special' agricultural college. Other boys were in small factory jobs or in shops and garages. The girls also were employed in light factory work or in shops. One with IQ 80 and a reading age of 8 was studying for O-level in art. One boy and one girl, both with IQs of 58, were not ready to go into direct employment; the boy went on to an adult training centre and was doing well in it, the girl was being trained at home where her mother was teaching her to help in the house and to do shopping errands. She loved gardening and there was a possibility that after she had matured further she might be able to go on to work with her brother in a firm of contract gardeners.

One's first impression on visiting the school is that it *is* a school. The children are friendly, socially at ease and busily occupied – there is a buzz of controlled activity in whichever room you visit. In the garden the boys' latest achievement is the erection of their own glass-houses. The girls have a flat in which they learn, by doing, the arts of housekeeping. The boys have an extremely well-fitted workshop including power-tools. The whole provides a powerful contrast to the first school for slow-learners which I ever visited. The visit took place towards the end of the war when conditions and staffing were difficult. The children sat in rows at their desks; each day they 'read' ten lines from a Beacon Reader and then carefully copied them out into a lined writing book. This was followed by an equally careful copying out of their name, address and date of birth. Afterwards, they all did precisely ten sums – either adding up or subtracting tens and units. This completed the 'academic' programme. Thereafter, enormous bags of rags were produced which the children proceeded to fray into piled heaps of threads – I never could find out what happened to the frayed material. However, in its day this school had represented progress. It was a pleasant bungalow-type building in good gardens, the classes were small in number and the teachers genuinely kindly and concerned. The children were happy because they were accepted and the demands made upon them were well within what was then believed to be their capacity. They were excellently cared for physically and were trained to do simple errands at the little shops which were in the same road as the school. The majority of them were also taught to travel to and from school on the normal buses, which in itself was no small achievement in war-time conditions. The difference between the two schools is a fair representation of the increase in knowledge and change of orientation which has taken place in the last twenty-odd years, and also a measure of the progress that has been made in special education.

Needs for the future

Nevertheless there is still much to do. Firstly, there is a need for even more provision to be made so that all children who need special education can get it and without having to wait for a period before a place is available. Secondly, there should be equality of provision throughout the country, so that no child's chances of special help should depend upon his living in the right locality.

Thirdly, more teachers should be given the opportunity to enrol for one of the courses leading to a diploma in the teaching of whichever type of handicap interests them. Two things mainly prevent this at present: one, the over-all shortage of money available to each authority to spend in this way; and the need to replace the teacher in the school while he or she is away on the course. The anomaly in this is that the more promising and able the teacher, the more difficult it is to find even a temporary substitute, and so their very ability lessens their chances of gaining further qualifications.

Further, there is a need to examine critically the present accepted categories of handicapped children. In connexion with this point an important development is taking place at present in the special schools for the handicapped. Official notice is now being taken of what has long been well known: namely, it is unrealistic to attempt to categorize and place children in special schools according to the official list of recognized handicaps. Too often this has led to a child being described in terms of whatever provision has been available, the inevitable consequence of which is that all special schools, with the possible exception of those for the deaf, the blind and the otherwise severely physically handicapped child, are in fact dealing with children who could have been equally well placed in one of several other kinds of special school.

Very few children have only one easily identified handicap. For example, a delicate child may well also be educationally retarded, emotionally disturbed, and perhaps have some specific minor physical defect, while many slow-learning children suffer from a variety of minor physical handicaps and can display behaviour disturbances. Even the children with severe physical handicaps such as deafness or blindness commonly have the associated additional handicaps of emotional disturbance and educational retardation. The situation is even more complicated as psychological disturbances can often have physical consequences and it can be difficult to decide which came first. A typical example would be an asthmatic child who might be disturbed because of his asthma or who might equally well suffer from asthma because he was disturbed. Similarly, the question might be asked whether a severely withdrawn child was so because he was suffering from deafness to some degree, or whether he appeared to be deaf because of some form of mental disturbance. Very often even intensive medical investigation cannot produce a positive answer in such cases; hence, we now know that it is not a simple matter to decide the correct special school placement by a child's primary handicap, or even to be sure what it is.

Deaf and blind children do need very special facilities, as do some children with other severe physical handicaps; therefore special schools designed to deal exclusively with them will undoubtedly continue to exist. Even when eventually other special schools are no longer categorized as schools for slow learners, for delicate children, etc., there will still exist, logically and practically, a tendency to select for the different schools children who appear to have special needs in common. Tests are already in existence which would make it possible to select on a more scientific basis. A great deal of the research in this line has been carried out in America and has resulted in such standardized techniques as, for example, McCarthy and Kirk's Illinois Test of Psycholinguistic Abilities.[4] Although this test is still being developed, even in its present form it gives a very detailed diagnostic profile of a child's learning characteristics and clearly shows in which areas his particular weaknesses and strengths exist. This information not only enables the remedial teaching programme to be specifically designed, but also can make the teacher's task both easier and more efficient at the same time as it enables the grouping of the children for teaching purposes to be geared to their displayed common learning characteristics as well as to their intellectual and physical abilities.

The difficulty of fitting children into the accepted categories has undoubtedly contributed to the schools being largely superseded by 'comprehensive' special schools which deal with a variety of children with differing disabilities. A very special example of this is the immigrant child, especially perhaps the West Indian. There is still a tendency for a quite disproportionate number of them to be placed in schools for slow-learners (see Barry Hill's article).[5] This tendency was sufficient to arouse concern three years ago but the hard fact is that very few Local Education Authorities have in fact done much to improve the situation. The problem seems to arise chiefly from the fact that very few of these children are given a sufficiently sophisticated psychological testing and assessment when they are first brought forward for advice and possible placement in special schools. Many of these children do have great difficulties in adapting to a totally new way of life and one with which their parents are also unfamiliar and baffled. Their language development is also sometimes different or retarded. If therefore, they are only seen by a School Medical Officer using the standard form they will appear to be genuinely dull and so be recommended for schools for slow-learners. In fact many have a much higher potential and needed only an introductory period in some special unit or class which would help them to adapt, and possibly, also some remedial teaching. The problem grows as very few of the children subsequently get re-assessed and very few of their parents who are privately able to voice their concern are willing or able to press the local authorities to look again at the suitability of their placement. It is a doubly unfortunate situation as every incorrectly placed child is not only being under-stimulated and inadequately educated for his own needs, but is also possibly occupying a place in a special school which is badly needed for one of the 10,000 children awaiting placement.

There is an obvious danger that official acceptance of the need for flexibility is nothing more than an act of recognition, and therefore only increases the tendency to place children wherever there is a vacancy available. This tendency regrettably, but understandably, increases when a child is particularly difficult to place for one reason or another. One solution is a great increase in specialist units, but these may be impractical since the greater selectivity of cases invariably leads to a smaller number of a particular case in any locality. Alternatively, different methods of selection for the schools could be introduced, based partly upon the diagnosed disease or handicap but mainly upon the child's diagnosed learning characteristics. This has been described as 'prescriptive education'.

We need a much more comprehensive system of after-care for children from special schools. This again is an area about which little is known. Jackson reports on a full-time research project which he carried out on 250 school-leavers in Scotland.[6] In the course of this research he critically examined many previous studies and found evidence to suggest that the greater number of them were too optimistic since they were usually confined to examining a relatively short period, from a few months to the first five years immediately after the pupil had left school. There was, therefore, little predictive value in these studies, since it was only after this period that other important factors began to operate. The five factors which Jackson considered to be most important were: the removal of the supportive home environment, age-restrictive employment, the effect of marriage and family commitments, the diminishing effect of supervision from after-care services and the effect of increasing age and mental handicap. Jackson also found that that there were serious weaknesses in the design of many of the published studies, which lessened their validity in assessing the adjustment of the school-leavers even in the initial period with which they dealt. He concludes that,

it should be re-emphasized that current assessments of employment adjustment have presented too optimistic a picture and that complacency will continue to be fed if attention is continually directed at such limited exposure to employment.

Prior to the Mental Health Act of 1959 all children who were considered by the school and the relevant medical officers to be in need of continued supervision after they had left school were reported to the local health authority under Section 57 (5) of the Education Act, 1944. The authority then arranged statutory supervision for these young people for as long as it was required. The number of cases which were referred in this way and the arrangements which were made varied widely in the different regions. Following the 1959 Act, all supervision became voluntary: in other words, the onus is now on the parents or their substitutes to seek supervision for their handicapped children if they feel it to be necessary. The arrangements made by the different local authorities continue to show wide variation. The best appoint either a social worker or a specially trained teacher to begin the provision for after-care in the last years of the pupil's school life, and so provided a familiar, sympathetic and knowledgeable adult with whom the young worker already has a relationship. On the whole, in most areas it is the special schools which assume the responsibility for maintaining friendly contact with their own ex-pupils. This is a good and effective way of providing after-care. However, it does mean that the teachers concerned, and the head teacher in particular, are undertaking a great deal of extra, frequently unpaid, work in the evenings and at the weekends. Where there is a social worker or a professionally trained counsellor appointed to the school this burden is considerably lightened. Apart from the continuing social care and opportunities, some slow-learners need and wish to attend evening classes for further instruction in the basic subjects. Ordinary evening institutes are not always suitable. Some special schools have also recognized this need and hold evening classes, and there are now evening institutes which offer special classes. Evening institutes combining teaching provision with the social opportunities offered by a youth club are probably a better solution than evening classes in special schools as there is a very normal and healthy tendency for the young adult at work to grow up and away from the wish to continue to attend his old school. This tendency may be even greater if he continues to be taught by his former school teachers.

As in all other areas there is a great need for more research. At present there are only general assumptions and firmly held views which have rarely, if ever, been put to experimental evaluation. Teachers and other professional bodies must learn to appreciate the value of such scientific validation. It is all too common to read or to hear of a good experiment which has evaluated a commonly held view being dismissed as a waste of time 'because we all knew that anyway before they started'. In fact we knew no such thing – we just believed it to be true partly because we had always heard it stated and partly because we believed we had proved it from our own experience without appreciating that we had not even been aware of the other possibilities which might have been in operation.

Appendix

The head teacher of a school for slow learners compiled the following list of the children in his school who had additional handicaps. The heads of special schools are preparing similar lists at present as their salaries are to be adjusted according to which handicap(s) is (are) decided, somehow, to be primary. The official intention was good; but it is already causing great problems because of the impossible task for head teachers and other administrators who are being asked to decide, before putting the names of children upon the lists, whether a medical officer would have considered any additional handicap sufficiently great to warrant the child's being excluded from education in the normal school. The complications and danger inherent in this are obvious.

Table 5 List of children with additional handicaps on a particular school roll as on 18 January 1968

Sex	Date of birth	Category
Boy	20.2.60	*Partially hearing* – congenital deformity face and ear; six operations Roehampton Hospital, further operations in future, under audiologist and teacher for deaf.
Boy	28.9.59	*Physically handicapped* – phenylketonuria; hand-tremor.
Boy	8.6.58	*Physically handicapped* – thoracic scoliosis, depressed sternum, lateral curvature of spine, receiving physiotherapy at Royal National Orthopaedic Hospital.
Girl	4.3.58	*Physically handicapped* – receiving physiotherapy.
Boy	23.3.59	*Speech defect* – dysphasia; *partially sighted* – cataract right eye; receiving speech therapy and physiotherapy.
Boy	24.4.60	*Speech defect* – idioglossia, has attended child guidance clinic and Queen Mary's Hospital, receiving therapy.
Boy	22.6.60	*Speech defect* – dyslalia, receiving therapy; *partially hearing* – low frequency deafness; *sight* – hypermetropia (long sightedness); seen at University College Hospital and local hospital.
Boy	20.2.61	*Maladjusted.*
Boy	18.3.61	*Speech defect* – receiving therapy.
Boy	9.12.58	*Speech defect* – therapy recommended by doctor, not being given.
Girl	20.4.58	*Speech defect* – dyslalia, stammer, receives speech therapy.
Girl	18.9.59	*Epileptic; maladjusted* – child guidance clinic.
Girl	4.6.60	*Maladjusted* – child guidance clinic.
Boy	8.5.57	*Physically handicapped* – receives psysiotherapy.
Boy	21.6.58	*Physically handicapped* – gross abnormal development.
Boy	18.12.57	*Epileptic.*
Boy	23.3.58	*Physically handicapped* – cerebral palsy, left hemiplegia, receives physiotherapy.

Table 5 – *continued*

Sex	Date of birth	Category
Boy	21.4.57	*Partially sighted* – bi-lateral cataract; *physically handicapped* – physiotherapy for scoliosis; *delicate*
Boy	18.5.57	*Epileptic* – seen at Queen Mary's Hospital.
Boy	13.2.58	*Delicate* – cardiac murmur.
Boy	14.2.58	*Maladjusted* – referred to local education authority.
Girl	3.3.58	*Partially hearing.*
Girl	7.6.58	*Physically handicapped* – receives physiotherapy.
Boy	11.7.57	*Physically handicapped* – cerebral palsy, receives physiotherapy; *speech defect* – dyslalia, receives speech therapy; has attended child guidance clinic.
Boy	3.2.56	*Maladjusted* – placement in school for maladjusted being sought; *speech defect* – stammer, dyslalia, dysphasia, receiving speech therapy.
Boy	14.8.55	*Speech defect* – dyslalia, receiving speech therapy; *phenylketonuria* – under Gt Ormond St Hospital.
Boy	27.4.56	*Speech defect* – dysphonia, slight hearing loss, receiving speech therapy.
Boy	4.11.56	*Physically handicapped* – bronchiectasis, kidney disease, receives physiotherapy.
Boy	14.11.56	*Partially sighted* – recommended school for partially sighted.
Boy	11.4.57	*Maladjusted* – child guidance for special tuition; in my opinion he suffers a mild anxiety state.
Boy	27.4.57	*Speech defect* – receptive dysphasia, receiving speech therapy.
Girl	25.5.55	*Epileptic.*
Girl	7.12.54	*Maladjusted.*
Boy	30.1.55	*Partially hearing.*
Girl	16.11.54	*Speech defect* – hypernasality and dyslalia, receiving treatment.
Boy	5.8.55	*Maladjusted* – four years at maladjusted unit.
Girl	8.1.54	*Physically handicapped* – heart condition.

Table 5 – *continued*

Sex	Date of birth	Category
Girl	7.3.54	*Physically handicapped* – right hemiplegia, receives physiotherapy.
Girl	1.9.54	*Epileptic.*
Boy	7.2.55	*Speech defect* – receives speech therapy.
Boy	18.12.54	*Physically handicapped* – minimal ataxic cerebral palsy and dyslexia.
Boy	11.5.53	*Partially hearing* – hearing aid, hearing nil right ear, severe loss left ear; *physically handicapped* – congenital heart, dwarfism; speech defect – cleft palate.
Boy	24.8.54	*Partially hearing.*
Boy	26.10.53	*Delicate* – asthma.
Boy	17.11.53	*Maladjusted; epileptic.*
Boy	7.2.54	*Maladjusted.*
Boy	2.4.54	*Maladjusted.*
Boy	11.10.54	*Maladjusted; epileptic.*
Boy	5.6.52	*Maladjusted.*
Girl	30.3.53	*Speech defect* – receiving therapy
Girl	12.3.53	*Epileptic.*
Girl	30.7.52	*Epileptic.*
Girl	7.11.52	*Speech defect* – stammer; *physically handicapped* – spastic, epileptic.
Girl	10.1.53	*Maladjusted; epileptic.*
Girl	23.1.53	*Epileptic.*
Girl	15.12.51	*Physically handicapped.*
Boy	3.11.51	*Speech defect.*
Boy	21.12.51	*Maladjusted.*

Part Four
Various Handicaps

So far in this book the problems of severely subnormal and subnormal children have been described and considered. With the aid of early diagnosis, family care, special education and continuing after-care, many of these children can become useful and happy members of the community at large; nevertheless they will always and inevitably be less able in differing degrees than the majority of the people with whom they live and work. The nature of their handicaps makes this inevitable. Certain things will always be barred to them; they will never enter any of the professions; they are very unlikely to become leaders in any kind of social or communal activity; nor will they become first-rate in any of the arts.

There are, however, some other children who function at the subnormal level and who would continue to do so if left untreated and in the exclusive and constant company of the severely subnormal, but who, with treatment, may function at much higher levels. These children have, until fairly recently, been classified as severely subnormal. Once they were so classified they were automatically regarded as ineducable and with a poor prognosis. In consequence the majority of them have spent their lives in the largely custodial care of mental or psychiatric hospitals or institutions. This has been inevitable because their care has imposed too great a strain on their parents and any other normal members of the family, particularly as all too often the parents have been unsupported by skilled and sympathetic help.

Continuing careful clinical observations and new research findings have now begun to differentiate certain children from the rest. This process has been speeded up and inspired by many of the parents who could not accept that their children were hopeless, and so devoted time and energy to drawing public attention to their needs. Many existing societies for helping the handicapped have also campaigned for them and have pioneered different forms of treatment. Following the publication of the *Health of the School Child* by the Department of Education and Science in 1960–61, which clearly stated that certain children previously deemed to be ineducable need not be assessed under Section 57 of the Act, local education authorities were empowered to make educational provision for these children, and more and more of them are now attempting to do so.

In this section of the book, these matters are further discussed and the different types of children known at present to fall into this category will be described. It must never be forgotten that for generations they have been undifferentiated from the severely subnormal. One is compelled to ask when sufficient money will be made available to enable time and care to be devoted to positive therapy and to research, both into the best methods of helping these children, and also in seeking to discover whether there are others who should also be differentiated from those children suffering from primary amentia or who are subnormal because of some form of irreparable physical damage. Each case left untreated which could have been helped to normality is a tragedy; the sum total is a national disgrace.

ChapterEight
Subnormal or . . . ?
Some Individual Studies

Every child born is unique, not only to his parents, but in actual fact. This statement is banal, obvious and beyond argument. However, while we recognize the truth of it we nevertheless expect babies to conform to recognized standards and patterns of development. Parents have always compared the development of their own children with those of their relatives and friends – and have rejoiced or worried in accordance with what they have found. The same process has been carried out on a larger scale and much more scientifically by experts such as Arnold Gesell and Jean Piaget – not to mention Benjamin Spock. We all establish norms of varying degrees of sophistication as to the ways in which we expect children to respond and to function at different ages. When a child who does not fulfil these expectations appears to be physically normal and intact, it is perhaps not surprising that medical, health and social workers suspect that the child is subnormal in intelligence. The suspicion appears to be confirmed if the child totally fails either to cooperate or to achieve a score above 50 when patient and skilled attempts are made to assess his intelligence. When this happens the parents are therefore warned that their child appears to be subnormal and that he will need to be educated in either a school for slow-learners or a junior training school.

Angela was such a case. She was the first child of very young parents. They married when the father was in Germany with the army and the mother came to live in England, which she had never even visited before, at the age of nineteen. She was six months pregnant at the time and spoke very little English. The young couple were determined to have a home of their own, although they were settling in the same town in which the husband's family lived. The only accommodation they could find was a basement flat under business premises near a busy main road.

It consisted of two rooms and was without a bathroom or a garden. Both parents, therefore, but especially the mother, were subjected to considerable stresses and strains from the beginning. Angela was born in hospital and her birth was completely normal. She was a beautiful baby and was successfully breast fed for some months. Her physical development was also normal. When she was just a year old, her younger brother was born and again there were no difficulties over the birth, feeding or development of this baby. Angela, however, acted as if he did not exist. As the children grew older, the difficulties imposed by their housing grew greater. The mother was an excellent housewife who kept the home spotlessly clean.

However, the family was always on top of each other and there was nowhere for the children to play. They had no garden, could not be allowed out on to the street because of the traffic on the near-by main road, and the nearest park was some distance away. There was also a growing disagreement between the parents about the children's up-bringing, especially Angela's, although there was no doubt at all that they both wanted and loved the children. By the time Angela was three she was presenting severe problems. Although she was very noisy and boisterous, she had no intelligible speech at all. She was wildly over-active and totally unable to concentrate or even to stay still for the briefest period of time. She still ignored or was openly hostile to her brother, and whenever she was frustrated or upset, savagely attacked herself or tore her clothes to pieces. She only slept with the aid of sleeping tablets and once had to be admitted to hospital for a day, because she had 'eaten too many of them'.

Her mother confessed to being completely at a loss to understand her, nor could she feel close to her. However, she was able to cope with the brother and could be openly loving and affectionate to him. She felt convinced that she must try to control Angela and attempted to be strict and to 'keep a firm grip on her'. The father was much more permissive on the whole with both children, although at times he could lose his temper and appear noisy and somewhat violent. He always felt unwilling to punish Angela as he thought that she did not understand her own actions and that she was incapable of controlling them.

The attempt to place Angela in a day nursery ended in failure.

At the local clinics the parents were warned that she was very backward and unlikely ever to be capable of going to school, but she might be able to go to a training centre at seven if she improved at all. At the age of five, although there was no improvement whatever in her behaviour and attempted speech, she was admitted to the local infant school but was completely excluded after four weeks. The parents were again told by a medical officer that she would always be unsuitable for school. She then remained at home and a regular weekly session with a speech therapist was her only teaching and training for a time. The parents could not accept that all her behaviour was that of a severely subnormal child, so, with the aid of their G.P., obtained an appointment for her to visit a diagnostic hospital unit for specialist opinion. The specialist agreed that she might have a higher potential, but felt that it would be necessary for her to be admitted to a residential diagnostic ward, since without this it was impossible to assess how much the very restricted life they were forced to live at home was contributing both to Angela's own behaviour problems and the growing difficulties of the parents.

Angela was finally admitted to a residential ward for assessment at the age of six years seven months. Even in this special ward her behaviour was so difficult and her attempted speech so unintelligible that she was not able to be taught on the ward, but went, as a temporary expedient, to the hospital training centre, which fortunately was very tolerant and understanding. The hospital psychologist did succeed eventually in completing a formal intelligence test which gave Angela an IQ of 48. However, she was proving to have great skill and originality in modelling with plastic materials, and for this and other reasons both the psychologist and the speech therapist felt that the IQ score might be an underestimate and that a lengthy trial in a special educational environment would be the only way to obtain a true judgement. She was therefore discharged from hospital and I admitted her to our special day unit for severely disturbed children.

It took us nearly a year to settle Angela into the unit. During the whole of this first year we made few attempts to direct her, since we hoped to find clues from watching her spontaneous activities as to how we could help her and also to discover what was going wrong with her noisy attempts to speak. Frequent contact was maintained with the parents and efforts were made to get them better housing – they had been on the council's list for seven years and understandably felt very despairing at times. During this settling-in period Angela did not have speech therapy, with the exception of a few weeks at the end of the first year, partly because there was no speech therapist available. However, it did become clear that she understood some speech and she became adept at finding ingenious ways to show her teacher that she had understood a word – for instance, one day she heard ice-cream mentioned and darted to the bookshelf where she found a book with a picture of an ice-cream cornet. She not only brought this to the teacher but also began frantically to pretend to lick the cornet as if to show that she not only understood the word but also its content. Similarly, on another occasion she found a picture of a windmill and again rather frantically blew at the sails then whirled her arms as if to demonstrate the same thing. Even at the end of the first year when she was beginning to react to adults she had no contact at all with the other children, who tended to ignore her. They were remarkably tolerant of her noise and frenzied activity. This was probably partly because all her destructiveness was self-directed; she never deliberately attacked them or interfered with anything they were doing and making.

During the second year, two important events took place – we finally succeeded, with the psychiatrist's help, in getting the family rehoused in a modern flat, and we carried out a lengthy period of intense observation during which we carefully taped all Angela's attempt at speech, while at the same time keeping complete notes of her actions. We then examined the two, and found that it seemed possible that she was only hearing or retaining the initial syllable of every word and that this was what she reproduced and with fair accuracy. To test this hypothesis we spoke to Angela very slowly and over-pronounced each separate syllable of every word. The result was dramatic and fully confirmed our hypothesis. From then on we always spoke to her in this way. Angela's speech became slow, laboured and distorted but intelligible. This soon led to improvements in her behaviour because she was no longer baffled, frustrated and angry. Previously it must have seemed to her that everyone was deliberately misunderstanding her since she was reproducing correctly what she had heard and no one understood her.

From this period on, her progress was slow but continuous. Her IQ score also reflected the improvement. Within four years of her admission to our unit, she began to attend a normal school for one day a week and it was hoped that she would gradually become integrated into the school. However this did not happen, to a large extent this was not because Angela failed, but because the school proved to be lacking in all the ways discussed in the previous chapter. Since we were all anxious that Angela should not feel rejected the decision was made that she should instead move to a good school for slow-learners which had the advantages of smaller classes and teachers whose professional experience and training made them more able to analyse and supply Angela's needs. It did mean that academically she did not achieve the level we had hoped for but in every other way she succeeded. Her art work continued to be so good that it was regularly selected for exhibition, frequently won prizes and was sometimes even sold. She has gained her gold medal for swimming and is so competent in the home that she frequently takes over 'to give my Mum a rest'. She is a happy attractive girl, looking forward to leaving school in the normal way. She intends to keep up her art in her free time by enrolling at the local School of Art. Eventually she may well be able to find a job where she can use her undoubted talents, in the meanwhile she is sensibly prepared to earn her living in some other way and develop her art as a hobby.

Derek is another child whose parents were told that their child was severely subnormal. He also had no speech but made odd grunting and burring noises. Unlike Angela, he was a puny baby, an only child who was born some years after his parents' marriage. Their home, like Angela's, was cramped – an upstairs flat which was a poor conversion of an old semi-detached house. They also had no garden, lived very near a busy main road which was also near a railway and quite a long way from the nearest park. As Derek grew the parents went to unlimited trouble to keep him from making any noise whatever since they feared that if he did, and the people who lived downstairs complained, they would be turned out of their home.

In his first years Derek had several spells in hospital because of gastric difficulties and recurrent bronchitis. At five he was speechless, undersized, could not dress or tend to himself and did not eat solid food, nor did he make any attempt to feed himself. School could not even be considered for him and, on the parents' insistence, it was recommended that he should be sent as an in-patient to a psychiatric hospital for assessment. It was nearly a year before a bed became available and during the whole of this time he remained at home. Because of his frequent illnesses and their need to keep him quiet Derek was completely protected, amused and shielded by his parents; his mother in particular devoted nearly all her time to anticipating and catering to his every need.

When he was finally admitted to the hospital it was established that he had no organic or physical defects which would account for his lack of speech and achievement. During this assessment period he showed that he had skill in handling constructional materials and in making up complicated jigsaws. He also became obsessed with spinning things and would flap his arms and buzz excitedly as the wheel or top whirled around. Formal intelligence tests were impossible to administer, nor could a firm diagnosis be made, although the suggestion was made that he might be psychotic rather than severely subnormal. He was therefore recommended for a period of assessment to our unit.

After a lengthy period of observation and careful physical investigations, we felt that Derek's under-functioning was a direct consequence of his upbringing and not of severe subnormality. We therefore initiated a programme which was aimed at teaching him and then compelling him to use all the skills he needed to achieve complete physical independence. Fortunately his parents were able to accept this, even though it meant a long hard struggle initially, first to overcome Derek's inertia and then his active resistance to having to accept demands being made of him, rather than having his every wish anticipated and supplied. Intensive speech therapy was also initiated.

The way in which Derek was encouraged to feed himself with

solid food exemplifies the whole pattern. Initially we continued to beat his food to a liquid 'pap' which we then fed to him in his own elaborately slow and ritualistic way. We then continued to feed him but only from a spoon and while he sat at a table in the same room and at the same time as the other children had their meals. His repeated attempts to push them away from the table and to demand close and undivided attention from the adults were quietly but firmly resisted. As soon as this was achieved he was carefully taught how to feed himself with the spoon and then left to do it. He was constantly encouraged at first, but never helped and if he firmly refused to do it, his food was quietly cleared away when the meal-time was over. He was so startled and furious the first time this happened that he not only made his first attempts at intelligible speech but also found a way of openly showing his anger by completely mixing up all the children's wellington boots. His rage was enormous when he was then compelled to sort them out and replace them – a task which he proved to be completely capable of doing! And so it went on – the pap was replaced by finely chopped solid food, the pieces were then cut larger and he was taught to chew them. A knife and fork replaced the spoon – then he was taught to cut his food up himself. The battle is still not quite complete, since we are now making the final demand that he comes and collects his own food.

Since this pattern has been necessary for every facet of his activities, it has been a long and hard task which has demanded the utmost patience, skill and persistence from his teachers, his speech therapist and his parents. However, the future is now much more hopeful for Derek – he is now capable of complete physical independence, his speech is intelligible, although he will continue to need speech therapy for a period, he can meet the demands of a small classroom and take part in such group activities as PE and music. He is also beginning to read and to respond to formal teaching. Already it has been positively established that he is not severely subnormal, his over-all IQ as measured by WISC Intelligence Test being 78, and that possibly he will prove to be of average intelligence, although, with his long, slow, restricted start, his needs will undoubtedly be better supplied in the carefully designed, less demanding environment of the special school to which he was transferred in January 1969.

Ned is another child who eventually came to us after his parents had been told he was severely subnormal – in fact they were advised at one point that the best thing they could do to ensure his own happiness and to relieve the strain on the rest of the family would be to apply for his admission to a mental subnormality hospital. His father described how during the train journey home, he held the child on his knee 'with tears running down my face' as he wondered if he dared resist this advice, since he did appreciate how greatly his wife's health was being affected by the constant strain of caring for Ned and at the same time meeting the demands of running the home and giving a full share of attention to their younger child.

As we got to know the family more it seemed as if Ned's earlier history might have played a large part in his disturbance. He had spent the first eighteen months of his life in Malaya where he was extremely happy and cared for by a trusted Chinese *amah*. Just as he began to toddle and to speak, his whole world was transformed: the family returned to the much less spacious life of suburban England; his dearly loved *amah* disappeared; his mother not only had to undertake his sole care but also soon gave birth to the second baby; his father was working very long hours in order to earn good money to enable them to buy their own house as soon as possible. Ned became extremely disturbed, so much so that he became terrified of even changing his clothes. When the family had to move again because of the father's work, he was so distressed that it was impossible for his parents even to persuade him to remove his coat and wellington boots to go to bed. He could only sleep fully dressed and surrounded by all his cherished possessions. Eventually he only seemed to feel secure if he knew he was locked in his room. Usually he was completely passive and unresponsive, but occasionally had frenzied bursts of activity when he threw everything out of the window. He used no speech, only grunts and gestures, and gave little sign of comprehending any. Needless to say, he achieved no score at all in an intelligence test situation.

We admitted Ned as an acute family emergency the day after our first interview with him and his mother – his father was ill at the time. For the first term with us he never removed his clothes, even to go to bed – nor even to be washed – and he whimpered or burst into tears if another member of the staff passed through his classroom. Eventually the sight of all the other children happily stripped off and playing in the sandpit and paddling pool helped him to allow us to get his clothes off. By this time they were very smelly and ragged, and he accepted the clean clothes which we put on him with what appeared to be relief when the time came for him to go home. For a period after this, though, he still insisted on wearing on top of his clean clothes his old, smelly, grey pullover.

During the next phase we all developed our powers of running! From having refused to leave a room without a panic disturbance, Ned suddenly began enjoying the delights of freedom! The moment he was unobserved, he was away – first all over our own building and garden, then out into the hospital grounds. As these are reasonably large, we had quite an area to cover! This phase also passed as Ned became very interested in all the different activities that were available inside the school. He began to enjoy looking at books and wall-pictures, and finally the great day came when he suddenly pulled us over one at a time, pointed at a wall-picture and mouthed the names of the different objects he could identify in it. An important factor in his improvement was the decision of his parents that the father should take a different job, which, while it earned him less money, meant that he could see a great deal more of the family and give the mother much more active support. Ned became demonstrative in his affection for them and also, rather to his younger brother's chagrin at first, began to assume the role of the older child. It was at home that Ned first was able to talk out loud and not just mouth his speech. Soon he became a talking member of a teaching group at school, taking part in some group lessons and oral activities. When he was still only seven he went with a school party to London using public transport all the way and also on a visit to Portsmouth. The family moved house twice more until finally buying and settling down in a fairly large house with a good garden. He took both these moves completely in his stride with no hint of a recurrence of his earlier difficulties. At nine he was ready to leave us. He is a delightfully normal, sometimes healthily naughty boy and a full member of a warm stable family group. He frequently rings us up to pass on his news and to ask about the children he knew.

These are just three of the cases who came to our unit after having been diagnosed as severely subnormal and unsuitable for education in school. There are many others. Graham was an adopted child whose mother still trembled years afterwards when she described a performance test he was given as an eighteen-month-old baby in front of a 'batch of students', after which she was advised to 'put him away in a hospital and try again, adopting another baby'. Graham did improve with her intensive care but was still very timid and backward when the time came for him to start school. When he was old enough to be expected to use the boys' urinals, he just could not face doing so and attempted to use the lavatories. This he was not allowed to do, so he endured agonies daily as he tried not to go to the lavatory at all during school time. He achieved nothing scholastically and finally had to be literally dragged to school, screaming, and at the same time began to show open dislike of his mother since she was the one who took him; so school was abandoned altogether until he came to us a year later. When he was nine and a half he was admitted to a normal primary school again.

There was Terry whose whole development was drastically affected when he had to have part of a leg amputated at the age of two, and whose parents were asked not to visit him subsequently in hospital because it would 'upset him'. He returned home like 'a stuffed doll' showing no response to any stimulation. Fortunately this type of incident is far less likely to happen now – but it did happen to Terry in the late 1950s.

These children and the others whom we have admitted were fortunate because they had parents who somehow were both able to fight for them and also to sustain the enormous stresses and anxieties of keeping the child living at home with them. We have had others with whom the outcome has been less happy and who did prove to be suffering from degenerative diseases or who were 'unable to benefit from education'. For some of them a residential placement has had to be found, but the parents have found it easier to arrive at this decision after every attempt to improve their child or correctly diagnose his condition had been clearly made.

However, there are other children whose natural parents opt out of their life at the beginning of it, or who simply cannot support the burden of living day-in, day-out, with a handicapped child.

Recently I visited a hospital where some of these children live. It is a good one of its kind. Nothing that is said in the children's stories should be interpreted as a criticism directed at the hospital. The wards are reasonably large and not overcrowded since only twenty children live in each one. There is, however, no possible way of providing any privacy for any of the children in them. The nursing staff are kindly, the doctors and various therapists concerned are constructive in their approach. All the children who are capable of it go out to school of one form or another for part of the day. Those children who have them wear their own clothes, and there are plenty of toys and other play materials available. Although one could comment on some of the ways in which the children's lives are organized because of the traditional hospital routines and practices, nevertheless on the whole they are happy and cared-for in every sense of the word. Among them, however, were some such as Trixie, Chrissie, Victor and Betty.

Betty is less than four years old. She is illegitimate and has never known her own parents. She has almost literally drifted from one form of care to another and possibly in consequence has not developed any speech; nor has she matured emotionally. She has never been diagnosed as subnormal, nor indeed as anything else, yet there she is, living in a ward which is basically designed for children who have been diagnosed as severely subnormal. Since she has been there for a longer period than anywhere else in her short life and since she is genuinely loved by the nurses, she is so acutely anxious if any stranger visits the ward that she weeps inconsolably and clings to the nurses in desperate fear that the visitor has come to move her on yet again. It has been possible to arrange for her to go to a little special class one morning a week, and already, even with this small allowance of teaching, she is proving quick and responsive and intelligent in the way in which she plays. The hospital doctors are deeply concerned about her future and the hospital social worker is trying to find foster parents for her. Even if she is successful, Betty's ability to adjust to living with them and to meeting the demands of normal life is lessening with every day she spends on the ward, and she will certainly suffer greatly when she is moved from the place where, for the first time in her life, she is beginning to put down roots.

Victor is a beautiful child, fair and delicate looking. He comes from a large but broken family. His mother had to go to work when the home broke up and, as he was totally withdrawn and non-communicating, Victor had to go into someone's care. Since he was diagnosed as possibly psychotic, there was no suitable provision for him in any children's home, nor could he be fostered. He was therefore placed in the only other provision available – a ward for severe subnormality. There he remained for nearly three years – remote, speechless but still quite unlike the severely subnormal children around him. After some years of effort, the hospital persuaded the local education authority to set up a special class for psychotic children, and Victor now goes to this class for part of the week. It is impossible to say whether he will improve there. What can be said at the moment is that, in spite of the genuine concern of the hospital staff, after three years in their care he is still speechless, still withdrawn and functioning on a slightly lower level than he was on admission.

Chrissie is nearly twelve, a tall girl who is approaching puberty. She also is a child whose parents have had no contact with her for years and who seems to have been admitted to a hospital in the first place for diagnosis. She was not talking so she was suspected to be psychotic. She had frequent moves from hospital to hospital and from ward to ward, and her full history is only being established now because a concerned doctor has set out to investigate it. In this way it has been discovered that she was diagnosed as being deaf and not psychotic, and was at one time fitted with a hearing aid, following which improvements were noticed. There are gaps in her history; sometimes six months between entries. However, at some time the hearing aid was broken and since she was moved on after this, she has been without one for three years. She appears to be settled and happy, and responds in a lively way when visited by people whom she knows. Her pattern of life has probably been established and, now her history has been uncovered, she is being fitted as soon as possible with a new hearing aid. Chrissie at least appears happy; Trixie is not.

Trixie is an epileptic child. She has *grand mal* fits which occur periodically and her behaviour is disturbed when she is in such a state. All her earlier intelligence tests put her above the level of severe subnormality, although in the dull average to slow-learning range. She was therefore treated as an educable child. She has full normal speech, can read and has responded to teaching. Unfortunately her disturbed behaviour led to her being excluded from the residential school to which she was sent by her local education authority. Her family find it impossible to manage her at home, so for three years she has been on the waiting list for admission to a Rudolph Steiner school. When she was excluded from the residential school an emergency arose, and as a temporary expedient she was admitted to hospital.

Since she is a patient in a hospital for severe subnormality she is only able to attend the hospital school, where she is not sufficiently stimulated and so becomes either very difficult and 'flops' hopelessly and unresponsively on a bench. Fortunately this aspect of her life and of the other three children may well be improved as a consequence of the education authorities taking over the responsibility for the school. Meanwhile her behaviour continues to show signs of deterioration. On admission she ate properly and cleanly, using a knife and fork. Later she either used a spoon or pushed the food into her mouth with her hands, as did some of the subnormal children with whom she was in close proximity for every minute of the day and night. She rarely spoke spontaneously or even to the point. Her measured IQ dropped significantly. Her doctor, who was deeply concerned, said that she saw 'the child almost visibly rotting before my eyes'. Trixie had to take anti-convulsant drugs for her epilepsy, and to enable the ward staff to cope with her periods of disturbed behaviour she was given a depressant drug in addition. Subsequently, horrifyingly, she began to dribble, as many of the children on the ward frequently do. She could still control this as I saw when the doctor despairingly begged her to stop. She also became very quiet and sadly responsive when the doctor talked to her and expressed the concern she felt and the knowledge she had of the life which Trixie was leading. After desperately seeking to find a better placement, she was finally admitted to a residential school, but the placement broke down as it was not possible to spare sufficient staff-time to attempt to help her meet the demands of the school in the initial period. She was therefore returned to hospital.

As has been fully discussed in the earlier chapters of this book, there are many ways in which improvements can and must be made in the way of life which we provide for all these children, and not just for those who are probably misplaced. However, to sit in the ward and savour the squalor and horrible stench of one of the communal potting sessions is a test of endurance when one is a visitor and at liberty to open the door and go out into the world outside. The question has to be asked: what must children such as Trixie be enduring who have known differently but who, because nothing else is available, have to live as members of such a community and take part in such activities?

In the cases of all the children described, the hospital is not only caring for them when no one else would or could, but is making active attempts to obtain better provision for them – so far, however, without success. Without the drive and endurance of their parents and the fortunate chance of a suitable educational unit being available, this could so easily have been the fate of Angela, Derek, Ned and the others. One thinks of the 1600 children being admitted yearly to the hospitals and the high percentage of them listed as 'cause of deficiency unknown' and one feels rather frightened, not just for the children but also for the effect it must have on everyone else who is concerned in any way with the situation as it exists at present.

There is now some hope that it will be radically altered as a consequence of all the new legislation already discussed in this book. The continuing problem may well be to ensure that the changes envisaged do take place and as rapidly as possible.

Chapter Nine
Early Infantile Autism

There are some stories common to the folk-lore of many countries. Among these is the legend of the changeling child. In these old stories a beautiful human child was stolen soon after birth by the fairies, who left in its place a child of their own. This child was sometimes described as being ugly, but more frequently as a dainty, delicate, fairy-like creature, who yet was totally cold and unresponsive to the despair of its apparent parents, for it brought nothing but grief and anxiety to them. Sometimes it cried ceaselessly and inconsolably, at other times it lay quietly for hours totally self-engrossed, again sometimes it was a voracious eater, at other times it required the utmost patience and skill to induce it to take enough food to keep it alive. It seemed indifferent to pain and pleasure, heat and cold, and never responded lovingly in any way to anybody.

One is tempted to speculate whether these old stories are not the first accounts of children suffering from early infantile autism, for there is a great similarity between them and the behaviour which is now beginning to be regarded as typical of these children. There is very little doubt that there have always been autistic children; nevertheless it was only in 1943 that the first account of the syndrome was published by Dr Leo Kanner, emeritus Professor of Child Psychiatry at Johns Hopkins University, Baltimore. He also first diagnosed the syndrome 'early infantile autism' in a further paper which he published in 1944. In these papers he stated that autistic children are those,

who show extreme aloneness from the beginning of life, and an anxiously obsessive desire for the preservation of sameness ... The common denominator in all these patients is a disability to relate themselves in the ordinary way to people and situations from the beginning of life. ... The case histories indicate invariably the presence from the start of extreme autistic aloneness which, wherever possible, shuts out anything that comes to the child from the outside. ... They reject reality, tend to brood, and become obsessed with small repetitive activities (p. 739).[1]

Clear though this description of the basic problem appears to be, it is unfortunately not yet generally accepted and the term 'autism' is used and interpreted in many different ways. Dr Michael Rutter of the Institute of Psychiatry, London, says: 'Confusion has been compounded by the fact that not only have some writers used different terms for the same conditions but also the same terms have been used for different conditions.' In 1961 a British working party under the chairmanship of Dr Mildred Creek, then of Great Ormond Street Hospital, produced a progress report[2] which attempted to clarify and describe the 'schizophrenic syndrome in childhood' which the working party selected as their preferred term for the condition. This term has now been largely discarded because it suggests by implication that childhood autism may have some link with schizophrenia, and there is no direct evidence to support this. In fact there is a very low incidence of psychosis in the near relatives of autistic children. For example, Dr Kanner examined the family histories of his first series of 100 autistic children. In all, 973 near relatives, i.e. parents, grandparents, aunts and uncles were considered and only thirteen of them were known to have suffered from mental illness. This is significantly low, being only a third of the rate found in the normal American population.

Nevertheless, although the term preferred by the British working party is not now generally used, their report has played an important role both in focusing medical and general attention on the condition and in making some progress towards uniformity of diagnosis in this country.[2] It outlined the now famous 'nine points' which the authors stated to be an 'attempt' to 'extract from the observed data those signs of diagnostic value which are most frequently seen.' In other words, it was hoped that the general use of these points might help in the early recognition of significant deviations in the development of infants and young children. They were not intended as 'absolute criteria in the sense that all, or any particular one must be present, nor were they designed for use as a rating scale'. The unanimous opinion was that 'the heart of the matter was the presence of an impaired capacity for human relationships'.

The nine points that the child displays were:

1. Gross and sustained impairment of emotional relationships with people. This includes the more usual aloofness and the empty clinging (so-called symbiosis); also abnormal behaviour towards other people as persons, such as using them or parts of them impersonally. Difficulty in mixing and playing with other children is often outstanding and long-lasting.

2. Apparent unawareness of his own personal identity to a degree inappropriate to his age. This may be seen in abnormal behaviour towards himself, such as posturing or exploration and scrutiny of parts of his body. Repeated self-directed aggression, sometimes resulting in actual damage, may be another aspect of his lack of integration (see point 5) as also the confusion of personal pronouns (see point 7).

3. Pathological preoccupation with particular objects or certain characteristics of them, without regard to their accepted functions.

4. Sustained resistance to change in the environment and a striving to maintain or restore sameness. In some instances behaviour appears to aim at producing a state of perceptual monotony.

5. Abnormal perceptual experience (in the absence of discernible organic abnormality) is implied by excessive, diminished or unpredictable response to sensory stimuli, for example, visual and auditory avoidance (see points 2 and 4), insensitivity to pain and temperature.

6. Acute, excessive and seemingly illogical anxiety. This tends to be precipitated by change, whether in material environment or in routine, as well as by temporary interruption of a symbiotic attachment to persons or things (compare points 3 and 4, and also 1 and 2). Apparently commonplace phenomena or objects seem to become invested with terrifying qualities. On the other hand, an appropriate sense of fear in the face of real danger may be lacking.

7. Speech may have been lost or never acquired or may have

failed to develop beyond a level appropriate to an earlier stage. There may be confusion of personal pronouns (see point 2), echolalia, or other mannerisms of use and diction. Though words or phrases may be uttered, they may convey no sense of ordinary communication.

8. Distortion in motility patterns, for example,

(a) excess as in hyperkinesis,

(b) immobility as in katatonia,

(c) bizarre postures or ritualistic mannerisms, such as rocking and spinning (themselves or objects).

9. A background of serious retardation in which islets of normal, near-normal or exceptional intellectual function or skill may appear.

Unfortunately, it is inevitable that the use of diagnostic criteria so described must result in individual interpretation of them, and subjective assessment as to the degree of severity of the symptoms. This is specially important in this case, for it is true to say that at some stage of his development every normal child displays every item of behaviour described in the nine points. For example, a baby in the first weeks of his life is completely self-motivated and without emotional relationships. Later he may spend long periods in his pram, happily engrossed in watching the movements of his own hands. The important difference is that these activities are temporary with a normal baby, whereas the autistic child tends to persist in them for long periods, often for years on end and to the exclusion of everything else. Between these extremes of the normal and the severely autistic is an infinite variety of degrees of severity and persistence, and each person observing them makes his own assessment. The consequence of all this is that in general it is still not possible to know whether the same condition is being discussed by different people, even when they use the nine points as the basis of their diagnosis. The situation is further complicated for the term 'autism' can be used both for a diagnostic group, or to describe a symptom or set of symptoms, and it is not always made clear which use of the term is being applied.

If anything the use of the term is becoming increasingly disparate as the years go by. Children with known brain damage (even as severe as epilepsy) – with differing degrees of deafness – with clinically established reasons for severe subnormality are examples of physical conditions which are frequently found among children called 'autistic' simply because they display some of the associated symptoms. This is as inaccurate as saying that every child with a temperature or a rash has measles. An even looser application of the word, is the growing practice of applying it to children 'with autistic tendencies'. We have now reached the position where anyone talking about 'autistic' children has first to describe how they define the term. One is forced to question the usefulness of the word where this is the case. The point has been made that accuracy of definition is unimportant as labelling a child in this way opens the door to special educational units. This has a questionable validity, but in my own opinion it is wrong for several reasons; firstly I can see no value in using a questionable label for this purpose, surely it is far more valid to make provision for all children with special needs; secondly there is a certain tendency in some quarters to make generalized and pontifical statements as to how 'autistic' children should be educated – if this is believed and acted upon for children with such a wide variety of handicaps as are sheltering under this 'umbrella' very few of them are, in fact, going to receive education suitable to their needs; and thirdly because it can cause an additional and totally unnecessary hardship to parents who accept this diagnosis hopefully, only to have to face the fact when more exact and careful diagnosis has taken place that their child has in fact, a different and possibly more severe handicap.

For these reasons it is still not possible to estimate correctly the size of the problem, and there is evidence for assuming that many autistic children are still being diagnosed as feeble-minded and possibly deaf. Nevertheless, even with the present degree of knowledge of the incidence, it is evident that the situation is serious. A recent (1964–5) survey of Middlesex school children aged eight, nine and ten, conducted by Victor Lotter and his colleagues in the Social Psychiatry Research Unit at the Maudsley Hospital, London, showed that there were 2·1 per 10,000 with the severe Kanner syndrome and a further 2·5 per 10,000 who displayed some of the features associated with childhood autism.[3] Assuming that these figures can be regarded as representative of the country as a whole, there are at present more than 3000 children between the ages of five and fourteen who suffer from autism, a figure which is only slightly less than the number of deaf children and more than the number of blind children. There is, however, as yet no comparable educational provision being made for the autistic children.

One of the many mysteries which still remain to be resolved about childhood autism is its cause. Many experts have propounded differing theories to account for it, but there is, as yet, insufficient evidence to completely confirm or negate any of them. Some of the earlier theories, such as those of the American psychiatrists, Bender who regarded it as part of adult schizophrenia,[4] and West who considered it to be synonymous with childhood asphasia,[5] are now considered to be untenable as they are not supported by the known evidence. Leo Kanner has produced some data which indicated the possibility of a psychogenetic factor. Other writers such as Rimland [6] in America and Wing [7] in England have argued strongly against the possibility and have quoted evidence to support their arguments.

There is a large measure of agreement that the main problem of the autistic child stems from his inability to utilize and to generalize from his perceptions and separate experiences. The cause of this failure is as yet unknown and it is clear that a great deal of research is needed before a comprehensive theory of causation can be formulated. Most of the present hypotheses are necessarily based largely on clinical observation, although some experimental work is now being initiated. In England, for example, Hermelin and O'Connor [8] are conducting some controlled experiments in such matters as sensory dominance and visual imperceptions, and Dr Ounsted, J. Hutt, C. Hutt and D. Lee have done some electroencephalographic investigations.[9] Ultimately the sum of these and other experimental approaches may lead to an understanding of the causes of the illness.

Meanwhile both physical and psychological hypotheses are being propounded in attempts to explain the causes. The physical explanation postulates some form of cerebral dysfunction, which probably lies in the central nervous system. Rimland in America, for example, has developed a theory along these lines.

He thinks that the reticular system of the autistic child is impaired and that this is the prime and sufficient explanation. However, more refined medical research is needed before this can be positively established. Nevertheless, this theory, or modifications of it, is supported by many leading authorities for it does provide a reasonable explanation for much of the observed behaviour.

For a stimulus to be completely perceived so that apperception (which is the term used to describe the integrating of separate perceptions into a meaningful whole) is to take place, certain things are necessary. The perceptual organs, the sensory pathways and the receiving and processing centres of the central nervous systems must be intact and functioning correctly. A breakdown of any one of these would prevent or distort the stimulus and such faulty physical functioning would inevitably have psychological consequences. In addition, apperception can also be affected by the conditions in which the stimulus takes place. This can be best illustrated from common experience. If, for example, a person is completely engrossed in an activity, such as reading, listening to music, or watching a programme on television when the door-bell or telephone rings, it is possible that it will either be unheard unless repeated or that it will be heard but that there will be a delay before the person who has heard it reacts to what he has heard. This phenomenon can be described as inhibition of attention and this may be precisely what is happening to the perceptions of the autistic child. In the example just quoted, the attention was focused on a universally understood external stimulus. The autistic child's attention may be similarly and exclusively focused on a preoccupation of his own which is either immediately observable, such as a stereotyped movement of the hands, or an apparently internal preoccupation which leads to a position of immobility and gaze aversion.

If this explanation is correct, a further question obviously needs to be answered, namely, why does the child so consistently withhold his attention or fail to respond to external stimuli? To this question again the replies are largely speculative. There is some evidence, notably in some of the experiments done at the Park Hospital, Oxford, by C. Ounsted and C. and J. Hunt, that the autistic child is in a high state of arousal during all his waking hours. He therefore cannot tolerate the intensity of his perceptions and so either responds by frenzied activity, or by 'freezing' all responses. The same child can show acute distress in response to a very small sound. It will be extremely useful if further research produces more evidence as regards this possibility.

A most interesting hypothesis has been put forward by Des Lauriers and Carlson, which involves both the endo-reticular system and the 'limbic' system.[10] In the normal way, all new experiences are perceived through the endo-reticular system, then are consolidated and become part of apperception, because of the pleasure or pain or other emotional concomitant of the new learning which is experienced through the functioning of the limbic system. The hypothesis is that if in any way the interlinking of these two systems becomes 'out of gear', so to speak, acute disturbance is the inevitable consequence. If the limbic system is weak, new perceptions are non-consolidated, which would lead to the sort of handicaps displayed by the autistic child; if it is too powerful then the consequence might be the 'marasmic' child, who becomes so totally absorbed in an emotional experience that he becomes oblivious to all else. In extreme conditions this could lead to death, as even such primary needs as eating are unattended to. In some ways this hypothesis is the most plausible of all so far put forward as it accounts most fully for all the observed symptoms.

Tredgold and Soddy have suggested that the key to causation lies in the infantile feeding satisfaction pattern of the child.[11] Normally the first external experiences of the baby are related to this, and also his first emotional experiences. From this develops his first rudimentary consciousness of self and awareness of environmental objects, notably his mother. Thus his first primitive satisfaction, namely relief from hunger, becomes linked gradually with the associated pleasures of cuddling, caressing, watching his mother, etc., and as he gets older these latter pleasures become more important. In other words, the focus of his satisfactions has shifted away from his own body on to an external experience. Tredgold and Soddy suggest that it is when this development fails to take place for one reason or another that the autistic pattern starts. They offer various suggestions as to why this may happen, and state that the consequence of this failure is that the child remains, as it were, imprisoned in his own body, which he fails to identify as a separate entity.

Goldie and van Velzer published in 1965 a paper which may have some relevance to this theory.[12] It described some research which they carried out on new-born normal infants at the Hammersmith Hospital. By means of clinical observations and simultaneous electroencephalographic recordings, they clearly established that babies not only have innate sleep rhythms from birth, but also that there are significant consequences of rousing the baby from the different phases of his sleep. If he is woken in the 'wrong' phase, it may affect, from the start, the whole of his interaction with his environment and also the establishment of a normal diurnal sleep–waking cycle, for he can neither feed easily nor with satisfaction, and is much more difficult to comfort and to settle back to sleep. Since it has also been established that an adult suddenly woken from deep sleep experiences dereistic thinking, i.e. thinking not adapted to reality, the hazy experience of things half-comprehended, it is possible to speculate that the baby woken in the 'wrong' phase has a comparable experience which is the cause of his irritability, and also that if this experience is repeated regularly because of an imposed feeding pattern it may have serious consequences.

The above theories indicate not only some of the many interesting discoveries which remain to be made, but also the highly complex nature of the whole problem, for it is an undoubted fact that whatever the initial cause may prove to be, the condition becomes complicated very soon by the varying reactions and emotions of everyone concerned. It is perhaps not surprising, therefore, that there are many differing approaches to the treatment of these children. It is highly unlikely that all autistic children will need or benefit from the same type of approach or that there will prove to be only one correct method of treatment. In one sense it is true that there is no possibility of finding a cure until the cause has been established, therefore there is no specific treatment for autism. Here again much experimental work needs to be done, so that the results of the different approaches may be fully evaluated. One such study is being undertaken at present by the Medical Research Council. So far there are very few follow-up studies, but those that there are all tend to show that children who have had any sort of special education do better than those either left untreated or treated in other ways. Michael Rutter states the position in this way:

In our present state of knowledge education probably constitutes the most important aspect of treatment and it is to school in one form or another that we must look for the greatest hope of bringing about improvement in the child.[13]

The education of autistic children is still in the experimental stage for, until very recently, it has been felt to be inappropriate even to discuss it. In consequence, each unit where they are being educated is, in a very real sense, a research unit which is engaged in working out its own approach. There is no one correct way to educate these children; in fact it is highly unlikely that this will ever be the case. Eventually it may even be proved that there is no separate and distinct illness of autism.

Nevertheless, there is undoubtedly a group of children who have many very severe symptoms in common, and there does seem to be universal agreement as to the two immediate tasks which must be undertaken by anybody who is attempting to educate them. Education in this context must initially be interpreted in the widest possible sense and not in terms of formal teaching. The first of these tasks is to help the children to establish their own identity and to recognize self from non-self. G. D. Clark, formerly of High Wick Psychiatric Unit, expressed it in this way: 'These children have to be taught to *be* before they can be taught to *do* (p. 36)'.[14] Sometimes it is possible to record the actual time when this establishment of 'self' appears to have occurred. Nicky, a girl of eight, who displayed the complete Kanner syndrome to a severe degree, and who had never been heard to use any speech, went into her teacher's room one day, after she had attended school for approximately four months. She stripped off all her clothes and then climbed onto the teacher's desk so that she could see herself in the mirror behind it. She then ran her hands over her whole body, looking intently at herself in the mirror as she did so. When she had literally touched and examined every part of herself, she said interrogatively 'Nicky?' to which the watching teacher replied immediately 'Yes, that's

Nicky.' She repeated the whole performance twice more, each time finishing with the questioning 'Nicky?' After the third time she urinated and again watched closely as she did it. She then climbed down, dried herself (and the desk) and put her clothes on again. She never repeated this incident, but from then on responded as she had not done before when spoken to by name. She also began to speak her name in appropriate tones whenever she badly wanted something or was in distress. Previously whenever she had wanted anything she took an adult's hand and used it as a tool, but subsequently she called 'Nick' or 'Nicky', and after she had secured the other person's attention in this way, indicated what she wanted.

The other prime necessity is the forming of a relationship with the child. The problem to be solved is an extremely difficult one. Some way has to be devised to 'get through' to a child who never looks directly at another person, for his gaze is always averted; who probably does not speak; who does not want to play or to use toys; who may have no interest in sand, water or similar materials; who may sit for long periods completely inactive or engrossed in watching the movement of his fingers, perhaps twiddling a stick or a piece of string; or who may have frenzied bursts of hyperactivity; who is not interested in food, even sweets, or who may be a compulsive eater; who either ignores or over-reacts to sounds; who does not react to heat or cold, pleasure or pain, who indeed may at times attack himself savagely in such ways as hitting his head against a wall or viciously biting or scratching himself; a child who, above all, appears to want no contact with another person however loving the approach may be.

At the present time two main ways of solving this problem are being investigated. One is based largely on a strictly controlled, highly structured approach. This has the advantage both of being based on testable hypotheses and also of being easily subject to experimental findings. The programme is determined and designed in advance by the teacher, and the child and his activities are controlled throughout by the adult. *Behaviourism* is the basis of this approach and *operant conditioning* is the method used. 'Correct' responses are immediately rewarded either by sweets or praise and expressed approval, while incorrect ones are immediately checked by expressed disapproval, punishment or the associating of them with an unpleasant experience. The most extreme use of this technique so far has been experimented with by Lovat in America.[15] If all else failed, he punished 'wrong' responses by the use of electric shocks. His cases were also selected compulsive eaters, so he was able to give immediate rewards or punishments by withholding or giving food. They must therefore be regarded as special cases. From the accounts, they were severely affected and other means of treatment had been tried without success.

In England no centre uses such an extreme form of operant conditioning. Severe illness may require drastic treatment and this can be justified by its success. However, carried to its extreme, this argument can also lead to excess. Clearly a decision as to whether to use this type of treatment can only be taken by a person in full possession of all the facts. The really difficult decision is probably to determine the point when it is reasonable to conclude that this is the only course still available. To me the most cogent argument against the general use of the behaviouristic approach in the initial stages of the teaching programme is that there is no possibility of rewarding the severely affected child who, as Peter Mittler says, 'is inert and motiveless, and above all unresponsive to incentives of praise, encouragement or reward.'[16] It cannot therefore be assumed that these children are accessible through the satisfaction of their primitive needs. It is also possible to debate the long-term value of imposed training, although it can undoubtedly produce immediate results. It could be subject to breakdown in different conditions and could also, by its nature, impose a limit on achievement.

The alternative method could be called the *empirical approach*, since it is based on the assumption that, in our present state of knowledge, it is not desirable to predetermine a programme, although the ultimate aim is obviously to enable the child to function as fully as possible in every way. This approach is eclectic, much more complex and much less intrinsically restrictive. Nevertheless, it does suffer from the disadvantage that it is much less easily subject to experimental evaluation, and is consequently vulnerable to the dangers involved in subjective evaluation. In this method each child is regarded as a unique case to be studied so that any clues which he gives as to his predilections may be utilized to help him. This is the approach which I use at The Lindens, the unit for psychotic and seriously disturbed children set up by the Education Committee of Surrey County Council in collaboration with the South West Regional Hospital Board. The children attending this unit are not all autistic since it is felt that autistic and other non-communicating children urgently need the company of verbally communicating children who, however disturbed, nevertheless do form relationships and follow normal childhood interests.

Initially the child is left free to follow his own pursuits in a large room filled with toys and other material. No pressures whatever are applied at this time since it is basically a period of close observation and of familiarizing the child with his environment. Repeated observations of different autistic children have established certain facts, many of which are confirmed by the reported observations of workers in other centres. They are as follows.

1. These children appear to comprehend most easily information which they gain by using touch and smell, for almost invariably everything and everybody new is smelt, handled and stroked. Frequently this exploration is confined to one part only of the whole, e.g. a shining watch strap, patent leather shoes, soft fur or rough tweed. This fact is a very useful aid when making initial approaches to the child since exploiting it helps to gain and focus his attention on another person. Perfume can be used and attractive materials of differing textures worn. A bright necklace, which swings as the person moves, or shining ear-rings are also useful aids for this purpose; the earrings are particularly useful for, if both are watched, as they often are, the child's attention is automatically focused on the adult's face.

2. Their hyperactive, or conversely hypoactive, responses are frequently evoked by their apparent inability to handle successfully the information which they receive through sight or hearing. It has been noticed that the children frequently shut their eyes at the same time as they are reacting to an auditory stimulus. Obviously this could be an indication of the fact that they are confusing these two senses; on the other hand it could be a deliberate extension of the inhibiting of their attention. One little

girl, after she had begun to speak, actually remarked as she deliberately turned her eyes away, 'I'm not going to look at you, I don't want to listen.'

3. They are very much more aware of what is happening around them than is immediately apparent; their typical 'gaze aversion' is evidence of this. It is also demonstrated if a child is determined to have something which the adult has taken from him. He does not immediately 'fight' for it, but obviously keeps the situation constantly under review and, the moment he thinks he is un-observed, will move extremely quickly straight to where it has been put and take it, even if as long a period as two hours has elapsed since it was removed. These children seem to alternate between using peripheral vision and a quick flickering direct glance.

4. Their comprehension of speech is much greater than their use of it. This has been constantly tested since it would be pos-sible to believe that a child had heard and reacted to a simple instruction when he had in fact reacted to other clues which had been inadvertently given. However, this becomes less likely as the instruction becomes more complex and involves going from one room to another and back. Incidents such as the following are supportive evidence. An autistic girl appeared to be completely self-engrossed in one corner of a room when two teachers ar-ranged to take another autistic child out for a social visit. At the end of school she was taken to her bedroom to be changed and dressed for going out. As they passed the other little girl's room, she came out of it fully changed and wearing her hat and coat. She took the adult's hand and led her to the front door. Although she had given no open indication that she was listening she demonstrated by her actions her complete comprehension, for she preceded and anticipated the necessary preparations.

Although these observations are utilized to the full, sometimes the only way to initiate responsive behaviour is to utilize and develop a child's preferred stereotype. In this way one child's aimless clapping movement was gradually evolved into a joint game of 'pat-a-cake', another, incessant twiddling of a piece of string became an enjoyed shared activity as she learned to thread gay beads on it.

In these varying ways a relationship slowly begins to form between the child and the adult. There is some evidence that a fundamental pattern of development then takes place. The child begins a series of 'temper tantrums'. However, although at this time he attempts to bite, scratch, kick and attack the adult, he is clutching him closely. This is followed by a completely spontaneous *recapitulation* of the child's earlier developmental stages. This is demonstrated in varying ways: for example, one little girl pulled a box into my room, placed a chair on another chair, put the box on top, then climbed in, pulled the top of the box down over her, curled up and began to rock. This was her sole activity for weeks on end. Two years later, long after she had left the box, another little girl who was a recent admission pulled a similar box into the room, put it on one chair only, climbed in in the same way and began to rock. A boy climbed on to my lap, curled up in a ball, began butting me with his head and announced he was going to 'start again'. Another demanded to 'go down'. When this was interpreted as a wish to be put down on the floor, he screamed 'no, no' and climbed up in my arms again. When asked how he wanted to go down, his reply was 'down by where the water goes'.

The next demonstrated or stated demand is for 'milk' and breast feeding. Here again this has to be shown very clearly by the child, before he is given a feeding bottle. As an example, one little girl pushed an ordinary milk bottle down inside my dress so that only the straw protruded at the top and began sucking to get the milk. Soiling and wetting also takes place, even if the child has previously been continent, and this may persist for months. In these ways the child recapitulates all his earlier experiences, but this time seems to be able to learn from them and to relate them into a normal perceptual framework. During this period, the adult is constantly interpreting his experiences to the child and structuring his environment. It has been found that this can be done by using whole sentences, although the child sometimes appears to comprehend them more easily if they are sung rather than spoken. Indeed, music in all forms seems to evoke a response and very often the first group activity the children really join in with is a musical game.

At the appropriate time we have found that speech does begin, but its development is highly complex and appears to depend a great deal upon the child's earlier history and experiences, including whether speech has been consistently used to him as a means of communication, and also upon such things as the amount of television, etc., that is watched or listened to in the home. It has varied from a child of eight beginning an infantile babble to another of the same age who began repeating the whole of the television news he had heard the night before.

Echolalia is very frequent. Even more commonly the child appears to speak on two levels producing echolalic sentences with pronoun reversal to express his wishes, such as 'Do you want to go in the garden?' meaning 'I want to go in the garden', while at the same time having to struggle to build up a vocabulary and learn to use it to express a wish or an idea which he has not previously had addressed to him as a question. The task here is to utilize the two forms so that the repetitive one becomes analysed and meaningful and then the words and sentence structure can be employed by the child in the construction of new sentences. We now feel that this is very certainly the point when skilled speech therapy is tremendously valuable to the child. This not only gives him practice in extending his relationships, but may very probably speed up his development in other ways.

From the point when speech has begun, the development of these children has followed the normal pattern although they can make very rapid progress in the later stages. They begin to form relationships with the other children and adults, take more and more part in group activities and games, and gradually begin to acquire the basic skills of reading, writing and arithmetic. Here the presence of the other communicating children is immensely valuable and a constant stimulation.

Now that some of our children have come to use full speech we are learning more about them. For example, we now have some evidence that they are not limited in their thinking in ways that have been previously postulated, for it is not merely confined to dealing with immediate concrete wishes or needs but they also begin to speculate with ideas, and to discuss and appreciate abstract concepts. Quite early in her development of speech, Daphne looked up at the sky and remarked 'I'll stay here, the sky's too big for me.' Mark, when seeing some crippled children, was acutely distressed and kept saying 'Those poor, poor children, why do they have to be like that?' Both of these children had tremendous difficulties in accepting that death was inevitable both for them and for the people they have come to love. Daphne also began to ask, when in doubt in any situation, 'Is that what a normal girl would do?' and, if so, would choose to do it. This positive attempt to appreciate and to conform to 'normal' standards was never openly suggested to her or even discussed with her until she spontaneously began to ask the question. Although she has not lived with her family for five years, she has also begun to describe some very early and detailed memories which her parents confirmed when we subsequently checked her account with them.

Operant conditioning techniques are used in this approach when they are deemed to be appropriate, in other words, when the child has become responsive to 'praise, encouragement and reward', has become fully aware of self, is forming relationships and is becoming aware of the limits which society will impose on him and the demands that it will make.

We now feel we can claim that our method of treating the children is hopeful. However, it is still too early to say more than that some autistic children do recover sufficiently well to take their places in the primary school and that some have now successfully transferred to the secondary school. Their progress needs to be followed into adolescence and adulthood before more can be said. The number so treated is extremely small as yet, therefore it would be quite wrong to generalize from them. This will not be possible until many more have been treated, and until the same basic approach has been tested out by other workers in other centres. As with so much else in this problem, there is a great need for research to be done into the best methods of educating these children.

It would not be appropriate to end this chapter without a brief discussion of the problems faced by the parents of these children. In one sense their dilemma is unique, for they alone have to face the task of living with a baby who in the vast majority of cases they have wanted, but who, from the very first months of life, appears to reject them and to be totally unresponsive to their offered affection. It is obviously essential for the person who later attempts to treat the child to keep this constantly in mind and to maintain the closest possible relationship with the parents. It may well be necessary at some stage to help them to tolerate the fact that for a while their child appears to give to the teacher all that he has not given to them, his parents. This was poignantly demonstrated on one occasion when an autistic girl ran towards her mother and her teacher who were standing talking together. This mother, like so many others, had spent years striving to help and understand her child in every way, and also in trying to get educational provision for her. She held her arms out lovingly to the child saying at the same time 'Hallo, my baby'. The little girl acted as if her mother was not there and threw her arms around the teacher, who had neither spoken nor made any move towards her.

Only too often the parents have had to cope alone with the implicit criticism of uninformed relatives, neighbours and the public at large, for there is nothing in the appearance of the children to indicate their handicap. They are usually physically perfect, often beautiful, and their sudden rages and total absorption in their own pursuits sometimes makes it appear to the casual observer that they are wilful and spoilt. The pity and sympathy extended to a blind or crippled child is not evoked in the same way by the autistic child. One of the most frustrating and difficult things to accept is the uselessness of the feeling they often arouse that 'normality is just around the corner' and that 'they could, if only they would'. It is not surprising that the ceaseless strain imposed on the parents by the attempt to continue to love, live with and help a child who in every way needs their continued care and tolerance but who appears to totally reject them, causes many of them to accept any placement which appears to offer the child security and the rest of the family the relief they so badly need. This is one reason why so many of these children are still being admitted to hospitals and centres for the severely subnormal.

Certain relatively inexpensive measures could easily be taken which would help to decrease the number so admitted. The provision of help for the mother in the home would be immediately useful. This could be provided in various ways: the extension of the 'home-help' service is an obvious one; alternatively, financial aid would enable the mothers to hire suitable help. This kind of provision has already been made in some Scandinavian countries and has proved to be invaluable in helping to safeguard the health of the mother so that she can continue to care for her child in the home. This help should not only be designed to cope with the actual domestic chores, but also to give the parents the opportunity to have some social life together, knowing that the child is being well cared for. The need for this kind of assistance is, of course, not only desirable for the parents of autistic children, but for every family trying to maintain a handicapped child in the home.

Appropriate educational facilities should be available as soon as the child reaches the earliest age when schooling can be provided, that is, when he is two and a half. It is not yet known whether early admission of the child will give him a better opportunity of improvement. It may be so, but on the other hand a certain degree of maturation may be necessary before improvement can be hoped for. There may be an optimum age for each child, which could depend on many factors, and this would not be the same for every autistic child. The chief advantages to be gained from early admission are that the parents are relieved of the care of the child for part of each day, and also that the child is in a situation which can offer him help as soon as he can profit from it in any degree.

Finally there should be appropriately staffed centres which offer the necessary facilities for family holidays. This is a desperate need and such provision should be an essential part of the health service and not left, as it is at present, to voluntary societies. Alternatively, this kind of help could be built into the school, as it is at The Lindens, which, although it is a day centre, has beds available. The families can thus have a holiday while the children stay without stress in familiar surroundings and are cared for by people whom they know.

At least 3000 children in this country at any one time are suffering from early infantile autism. This fact alone would justify, even compel, the financing from public funds of any kind of treatment and research which could help to mitigate the problem.

Ultimately, however, the lessons learned in the attempt to help these children will prove to be of advantage to all children, since there will inevitably be a wider application of all that is discovered.

Chapter Ten
Provisions for Children with 'Brain Damage'

From quite early times, one of the devices we have used to give information about objects has been to attach a label to them. We also use labels figuratively when we wish to classify persons and things. These labels can be used to indicate or classify a very wide group which has a common factor, or to describe one very particular group. The more select the group, the more it is important to confine the use of the label to objects or persons which strictly conform to the distinguishing features of the group. This careful use of specific labels should be very strictly adhered to when one is discussing various conditions or syndromes of behavioural, emotional or physical disturbance. Unfortunately this is not always the case and then the 'label' leads to confusion and, far from simplifying communication, actually leads to many complications.

In the previous chapter, this is illustrated by the various current uses of the term 'autism'. The use of the term 'brain damage' is another case in point. It is in no way a useful or helpful statement for a doctor to tell a parent or a teacher that a child is 'brain damaged' for this usage is so loose that it can only lead to alarm and unnecessary confusion. It also appears to indicate that there is one specific syndrome or defect and that it is possible to make a sharp and clear-cut distinction between the 'brain damaged' and the 'normal'. In fact, neither of these is correct. As with the other conditions which are discussed in this book, there is a continuum of 'brain damage' which ranges from severe abnormalities and clinical disorders resulting from disease, defects or lesions of the brain, to conditions which are only suggested by the observed behaviour of the person who is being considered.

At present there are three different ways in which the term 'brain damage' is being generally used. The first is strictly correct, but perhaps unnecessarily restrictive, for it reserves the use of the term to the severe disorders, as, for example, cerebral palsy or spasticity which is a dysfunction due, possibly, to birth injury, genetic or environmental causes, accident or disease.

The second goes to the other extreme and uses the term widely and indiscriminately, often to describe a certain type of behaviour. This use is incorrect: although some children who have brain damage do behave in this particular way, so do other children for other reasons; moreover, the converse is also true, for many children with known brain damage do not show this behaviour.

The third is correct and has some value since it is used to describe collectively many different varieties of disorder which have the common factor that they are all known to be the result of damage or dysfunction of the brain. However, by itself it is of little practical value. It is much more useful to know the extent and severity of the dysfunction, the cause of the damage, the age of the child at the time when the damage occurred, the exact part of the brain which is affected, as this will have great relevance to the consequences, and also whether the damage is causing an abnormal functioning of the part concerned or is preventing that part from functioning at all.

The manifestly abnormal conditions have been classified as cerebral dysfunctions, and of these the two most common are cerebral palsy and epilepsy. Cerebral palsy may be defined as,

a persistent but not unchanging disorder of movement and posture resulting from a defect or lesion of the immature brain. It may be associated with intellectual subnormality, epilepsy, sensory disorders or disturbances of emotion and personality, all having the same origin but affecting the patient to differing degrees.[1]

Although there are several varieties of cerebral palsy, there is nearly always some degree of weakness of the limbs or some degree of paralysis. The actual incidence of cerebral palsy is surprisingly high since about one child in every 300 has it in some degree One-quarter of these children are able to be educated in the normal schools, over a third are also severely subnormal, and approximately another third have minor associated handicaps which necessitate special schooling.

There are many forms of epilepsy, but the two most common forms are 'major epilepsy' or *grand mal* and the variety known as *petit mal*. In the first kind the patient is subject to attacks which lead to loss of consciousness during which he falls to the ground, becomes rigid and may have jerky movements of the arms and legs. These attacks last for differing periods but on average for five to ten minutes, and frequently followed by a period of sleep.

In *petit mal* the duration of the attack is much shorter, usually for a few moments only, and consists of what has been described as a 'blanking out' – in other words, the patient experiences a momentary lack of contact but does not fall, becomes rigid or has the convulsive limb movements associated with *grand mal*.

The incidence of epilepsy is even higher than that of cerebral palsy since nearly one child in a hundred has it in one form or another. Only about one third are considered to require special schools. However, this figure may need modification in the light of the comprehensive survey carried out on the Isle of Wight, which produced evidence that one quarter of the children in the normal schools who had either epilepsy or cerebral palsy were having severe difficulties in learning to read; they were reading at a level at least twenty-eight months behind that expected on the basis of their age and I Q.[2]

The lesser degrees of disability are those which do not necessarily involve definite abnormalities of function, but in which there are limits or delays in the development of normal functions. As it cannot be assumed that cerebral injury is the prime aetiological factor in all cases, these are, it has been suggested, much more correctly called minimal cerebral disorders rather than brain 'damage'.

These disorders would include the following disabilities which could all lead to poor educational functioning and possibly emotional and behavioural difficulties.[1]

1. Defects of vision and hearing, the minor degrees of which may be undetected by routine tests.

2. Minimal cerebral palsy which might result in 'clumsy behaviour'.

3. Apraxia and agnosia. Apraxia denotes an inability or a difficulty in manipulating or carrying out intended movements of

objects, although there is no defect in the motor mechanisms. Agnosia denotes an inability to attach meanings to sensory impressions and is often confined to one sensory pathway: a person who is not organically blind but who has visual agnosia cannot recognize objects by sight, but could identify by touch.

4. Perceptual disorders. These disorders are more comprehensive in effect than agnosia which is confined to one sense, and are common in spastic cerebral palsy. Recent work suggests that prematurely born babies are more likely than full-term babies to have such difficulties.[3]

5. Visual motor disorders which lead to uncoordinated limb and body movements.

6. Spatial and lateralization difficulties.

7. Disorders of body image.

In addition, a child affected by any one or a combination of these, is likely to develop secondary disorders of behaviour which might be the result both of his own frustrations and the reactions of his parents, teachers and the other children with whom he comes into contact. Such combinations can obviously lead to severe underfunctioning.

It is apparent therefore that many children with cerebral dysfunctions and minor lesions will need special educational treatment if they are not to function below their intellectual potential. Perhaps, even more important, their parents and teachers need to be given as full and accurate a diagnosis as possible so that they may be aware of the child's difficulties and problems, and hence more able to tolerate them with sympathetic understanding.

On the whole, the child with epilepsy can be educated within the recognized systems. Many, approximately 60 per cent, attend the normal schools – others go to schools for slow-learners. A few epileptic children go to one of the special boarding schools which are an integral part of a medical treatment centre. Lingfield in Surrey is the largest and best known of these. It is a private school but many local education authorities pay the fees of the children who are recommended to be sent there. Some epileptic children are also severely subnormal and if they live at home attend the junior training schools. Frequently they are found in the 'special care units'. The rest are mainly to be found in the mental deficiency hospitals and institutions.

It seems that the disturbed epileptic child is the one who is least provided for at present. Such children are extremely difficult to live with (as of course are many other handicapped children) and, therefore, if the parents do try to keep them at home, they often need more active assistance than they can obtain at present. If it proves impossible for the family to contain them, they are frequently unacceptable to the boarding schools also, particularly if they are violently aggressive in their disturbed phases. Their progress then follows the sad inevitable course: extensive, frequent rejections tend to increase and further complicate their original problems and to affect adversely their level of educational and social functioning. This is why all too frequently they – like Trixie whose placement was discussed earlier – are to be found in mental hospitals and subnormality institutions, since no other place is available. They are then liable to be affected by all the limitations of life in such environments and in addition frequently have to be kept sedated by drugs so that they can be contained in a ward of twenty children (all of whom need personal attention) which is often understaffed. Special boarding schools or hostels with careful medical supervision forming an intrinsic part of their organization would be more suitable for these children. Such schools could be provided if several local education authorities combined their resources to cater for all the children in their areas.

The children with cerebral palsy [4] are nearly all physically handicapped to varying degrees. There has, therefore, been much discussion as to the best type of educational provision for them. Obviously there is no one answer to this question; it must be related to each individual child's needs, intellectual potential and degree of handicap. The children require physical treatment especially in their earlier years; physiotherapy is therefore essential, as is skilled teaching aimed at developing speech and language. Without this active stimulation at an early age they become even weaker physically and very backward. Bowley says:

Bearing in mind the difficulties in generalizing ... it can be suggested, however, that the mental health of the handicapped child depends on the degree of acceptance he experiences in his family and his school setting, on the realistic appreciation of his physical limitations by his parents, his teachers, and by himself and on the practical and academic skills he learns to achieve. He needs support but he also needs stimulation.

In his early years he needs a rather more sheltered environment than an ordinary child, an environment which provides him with physical treatment as well as pre-school education.[5]

This is what he needs and if he is fortunate enough to live in an area where such provision is available he will benefit accordingly. Once again, though, it is clear that there is no uniformity of provision throughout the country. The Spastics Society has done a very great deal both to set up provision and to discover the children's needs; nevertheless there is still a tendency, as has been stated, for the worst-affected children to go to the mental sub-normality hospitals. Their stay in them is frequently prolonged unnecessarily because there are not enough residential schools available. This again subjects them to the dangers of deterioration which have already been discussed.

It is extremely difficult to obtain an accurate assessment of the true potential of a severely handicapped, cerebral palsied child. As Gardner and Johnson point out:

There are two main difficulties facing even the most experienced psychologist when he is called on to assess the learning abilities of cerebral palsied children who have severe multiple handicaps and considerable retardation. Firstly there is the difficulty of establishing communication with a child whose speech is minimal, whose hand control is limited, who is distractable, who may, in common with 16 per cent of cerebral palsied children, have a significant hearing loss or a subtle defect of vision and visual control, or who may be emotionally disturbed. . . .

Secondly there is the extreme difficulty of judging the effects of the deprivation of experience these children with severe multiple handicaps have almost inevitably suffered.[6]

The Spastics Society therefore set up a long-term assessment and experimental centre at Hawksworth Hall in 1957, for the 'borderline' children, estimated at approximately 10 per cent of the whole, who on short-term assessment were rated as of 'doubtful educability'. It was found that, with the benefit of educational help and a long-term assessment, just under one-half of the children were found to be educable. The significant statement is also made: 'We were often left with the impression that mental test score increases might have been more general had the educational help been given over a long period and started much earlier in the child's life.' At Hawksworth the children are admitted between the ages of five and fourteen, three-quarters of them being between seven and eleven. The conclusions to be drawn from the findings of this report are obvious.

It is estimated that the total number of cerebral palsied schoolchildren is between 11,250 to 13,800. Of these not less than 2500 are probably severely subnormal, of whom about 1500 are likely to benefit from special training.

Many of these children remain at home with their parents and go to day centres, junior training schools or special units for cerebral palsied children where these are available. Unfortunately there is not nearly enough of the right kind of provision available throughout the country as a whole and often even where some form of education is provided, there is no physiotherapy available.

Many families find that they cannot support indefinitely the almost intolerable burden of living with a multiply handicapped child. There is therefore a constant need for residential provision. Once again the Spastics Society has pioneered the setting up of such provision, other than in the traditional institutions. In May 1966 they opened their first residential unit for severely subnormal spastic children aged from seven to twelve at Meldreth in Cambridgeshire. The unit is planned very largely on the application of Professor Tizard's findings in the Brooklands experiment which were described in chapter 3. It was therefore designed to provide 'education training and therapy in conditions that were as near as could be to those of a family home, and an objective was to enable the children to achieve as great a degree of independence as possible'.[7] The syllabus aims to provide social education and is 'designed to stimulate emotional development, self-help, communication with others and occupational activities and to provide such general education as the child can absorb'. It is interesting to note that the centre is also specifically designed to avoid the three main dangers which are listed:

1. Letting the children vegetate without setting clear objectives for them;

2. 'Playing at school' with efforts to teach the rudiments of the three Rs and the creation of an artificial classroom atmosphere;

3. Treating the children as 'Rhesus monkeys', i.e. as laboratory subjects for research workers.

This last point should not be interpreted as a rejection of properly conducted research; in fact it is envisaged that the whole work of the unit will, in a very real sense, be a research programme which will involve the closest possible cooperation of all the members of the staff who will thus combine their training in various disciplines. One can only applaud and re-echo Loring's closing sentences in this article. He points out that the total cost of Meldreth will be a great drain on the Society's resources but concludes,

... if this expenditure upon a unique pioneer project achieves in careful research and accumulation and dissemination of knowledge what it is intended to achieve, the benefits to the children at the unit and to all mentally handicapped children may be great indeed. They are of an order that cannot be measured in money alone.

Junior training schools, special classes and other schools have been examined earlier in this book. They will not therefore be further discussed in this chapter, except to mention that many of the better training centres now have special-care units which are specifically designed for these and other multiply handicapped children. It is outside the scope of this book to discuss at any length the provisions made for the spastic children who are not so severely affected but it is interesting to see what provisions are made. As part of a research project Dr Bowley, the consultant psychologist to the Centre for Spastic Children at Cheyne Walk, Chelsea, investigated the placements of 104 educable children, ninety-six of whom had at the time left Cheyne Walk between the ages of five and seven. The results were as follows:

Table 6

Placement	Number of children
Still attending centre	8
Could not be traced	1
Attending training centres	2
Day schools for physically handicapped	52
Residential schools for physically handicapped	4
Schools for the deaf	3
Residential hospital schools	10
Residential Spastics Society schools	5
Residential private schools for spastics	2
Ordinary day schools	14
Ordinary day grammar school	1
Private Montessori school	1
Army school abroad	1

It will be seen from this that by far the greatest percentage were placed in day schools, and that those for the physically handicapped predominated.

Dr Bowley did find suggestive evidence that:

Cerebral palsied children, especially hemiplegics (i.e. children who have lost the ability to make voluntary movements on one side of the body) with above average intelligence, good verbal ability, and with no marked perceptual problems or additional handicaps of vision, or learning, or epilepsy, appear to be able to make a really satisfactory adjustment to a normal school without undue strain and to maintain a good scholastic standard.[5]

A more recent survey has been published which found evidence that, although mildly handicapped children of average intelligence could be transferred to ordinary schools after an initial training period in a nursery unit of a special school, their chances of success were improved if their transfer was delayed until they had acquired skill in reading and writing.[8] There was improvement also if, on first moving, they went to the reception class even if they were older than the rest of the children in this class. The authors strongly advocate the provision of more remedial teaching classes in the ordinary schools and also that the teachers actively concerned with the handicapped children in these classes should always be given copies of the full reports available which explain each child's specific physical and educational difficulties. This is so logical and sensible that one can only marvel at the fact that it is necessary to stress and advocate it. The concluding words of this article are also important and suggestive.

If teachers in ordinary schools realized from the beginning that the child's basic level of intelligence was at least average then there would be less possibility of the spastic child drifting into the educationally subnormal category and ending his school career as a failure.

Finally, the group of spastic children who are, at present, least adequately provided for are the severely handicapped intelligent children, especially those who not only have impaired hearing and little or no speech but who also have little control and effective use of their hands. They have such limited means of expression of their possible comprehension that it is little wonder that they have been considered ineducable for as long. They need such intensive individual therapy from many different specialists that day hospitals appear to be their best placement. It may also prove to be that the most important transforming feature in their education will be further developments of highly sensitive electronic remote controlled equipment such as the POSSUM (patient operated selector mechanism) typewriter and other similarly controlled devices.

The children with minimal cerebral lesions form a group which plainly demonstrates the advantages to be gained from as clear and explicit a diagnosis as can be arrived at; once this is obtained, two main consequences can be expected. In the first place both the child and his parents can benefit psychologically: the parents because they are then more able to appreciate and understand their child's difficulties and needs; the child, even if he is not able to understand his own difficulties, from his parents' increased tolerance and constructive help.

The story of Ruth illustrates this. She is the younger by several years of two children. The parents are both in professional occupations and their whole social circle is composed of families like their own where the children are intelligent and able, and tend to follow the pattern of grammar school, university, and entering a profession. The older child is very happily and successfully following the tradition. Ruth, although obviously intelligent and with a façade of social competence, nevertheless proved to be a great problem and a failure from the time she first went to school. She was very clumsy and awkward, her work was hopelessly untidy and, under the stress of continued failure, her apparent emotional maturity and social competence broke down. Ultimately, her behaviour became so disturbed and bizarre, and her educational achievement was so poor compared with her potential as measured in verbally orientated intelligence tests, that she was in danger of being excluded from school.

The whole family situation was becoming very involved and complex, the parents could not understand 'what had gone wrong'; nor could Ruth, who was also very ambivalent. On the one hand she could not envisage any other acceptable mode of living and education than the established family pattern, but on the other she knew she was failing in it and that far from going triumphantly through school as her elder sister was doing, she was in danger of being excluded altogether. Moreover, she was not even sure that she wished to follow the pattern. She had no friends and hated the teasing, good-natured though it frequently was, that her clumsy actions and rather volatile emotional behaviour provoked. She could not succeed in games or in any activity that involved motor manipulation. Her attempts to impress by 'lining-up' with adults and displaying in a rather supercilious, patronizing way her fund of general knowledge, information and excellent vocabulary, only gained her the reputation of being a show-off. At home she succeeded better in achieving the family standard as she was not involved there to the same degree in the things in which she always failed at school. The parents, therefore, understandably, were inclined to feel that many of her difficulties were provoked by the school.

Finally, Ruth was recommended to attend a child guidance clinic and from there was sent on to our centre for a period of observation and diagnosis. Repeated observations of her behaviour and a comprehensive account which we obtained from the hospital of her birth, led to the suspicion that her problems might initially have been physical in origin. She was therefore sent as an in-patient to a children's hospital for an intensive paediatric and neurological investigation, at the conclusion of which the paediatrician was able to diagnose that she was in fact a case of minimal cerebral palsy. Obviously, Ruth still needed a great deal of individual help and attention, but the whole situation was considerably eased for her and her parents, since they had received an authoritative answer to their query 'what went wrong?' Ruth eventually started full-time attendance in boarding school for children of above average I Q in September 1968.

Explicit diagnosis can lead to a precise understanding of each child's particular strengths and weaknesses which will greatly ease the teacher's task and enable him to plan his therapeutic and remedial approach much more efficiently. Unfortunately, the very loose use of the term 'brain damage' and the rather limited general understanding of the complexities of the problem still lead all too often to whole groups of children being put through activities and exercises for such reasons as 'brain-damaged children need to touch and feel around lots of shapes' or 'brain-damaged children need lots of such motor activity like crawling through hoops and shapes and things – it improves their body image'. I have heard both these statements made in recent lectures and certainly there is a little truth in them. Some children with particular disabilities, such as those with visual agnosia, may learn more easily in the first place through a sense different from sight, and some children with disorders of body image and spatial and lateralization difficulties will improve their body schema if they are given carefully designed and continuous visual, labyrinthic, tactile and kinaesthetic experiences. However, this is no justification for teaching a whole group in these ways regardless of each child's individual problems.

Although we are really only at the beginning of devising techniques for exact requirements, nevertheless we are already able to determine by means of the tests at present available both the child's probable weaknesses and also his learning characteristics. Comprehensive tests, such as the Wechsler Intelligence Scale, do not only give an over-all score, but also enable an estimate to be formed of particular aspects of the child's level of functioning. Discrepancies between the scores obtained, for example, on the verbal scale as compared with the performance scale, indicate strengths and weaknesses. Clinical investigations can detect the less gross physical handicaps.

Recently there has been a great deal of psychological research aimed at establishing and generalizing learning behaviours, and also in formulating techniques for the diagnosis of learning abilities and disabilities. Much of this work is being carried out in the USA; a typical example is the Illinois Test of Psycholinguistic Abilities.[9] These tests are still being critically examined and revised, but they do enable a profile to be drawn up for each child, which demonstrates his differing scores on a representative level and on automatic sequential tests, when the tasks are presented in auditory, visual, auditory-vocal, visual-motor, vocal and motor forms. This enables the child's strengths and weaknesses in interpreting and understanding through these different sensory pathways to be measured, and some controlled experimental work has already demonstrated what dramatic improvements can be achieved if the child's remedial programme is based on these findings. It is possible that in time classifications according to learning characteristics will replace categorization according to disease or disturbance in all special education, and that it will lead both to better results for the children and a more economic and efficient use of the teachers' time. Other research workers are concentrating on developing tests of specific learning disabilities in visual perception and language development.

All these projects will undoubtedly simplify the remedial teachers' tasks in the future. Meanwhile much of the work being done is still based on observation and trial and error following a rough assessment of a child's ability in the auditory and visual channels and the ability in perceptual-motor skills. Children with minimal cerebral lesions can be severely handicapped educationally in consequence. It is a far more difficult task to devise teaching techniques to enable them to overcome or compensate for these difficulties than it is to teach a severely disturbed or even psychotic child who is recovering from his illness or his disturbance.

In teaching these children it is necessary initially to exploit the sense by which they are most able to comprehend and interpret their experience. However, at the same time, it is also essential to use this preferred sense as an aid in developing the weaker senses. Although in our unit we cannot claim to have definitive answers yet how this can be achieved, we have found, as have other workers, that simultaneous presentation in various ways, and practice using different media, is beneficial. Peter, who was mentioned earlier in this book, was a child who had great difficulties in learning to read as a consequence of his minimal cerebral lesion. He achieved at a much faster rate when he both invented and then wrote with his teacher his own first reading books. The teacher then recorded on tape each separate page so that he could practice independently by using the tape-recorder. This helped him both to learn from the written page since he could frequently go over each one and also to check his achievement. In September 1968 he left to attend a normal primary school, initially attending a tutorial class for extra reading practice. This became no longer necessary, and he moved on to a normal secondary school in September 1969.

The talking typewriter is an extremely expensive teaching aid which exploits two or more senses simultaneously. The language-master is another useful, much cheaper aid. All of these will probably assist greatly in the teaching of children with specific learning difficulties. We have also found that the child with visual-motor problems and spatial lateralization difficulties can be saved a great deal of frustration if he is taught, as he can be, to use a typewriter, since this automatically both lines up and clearly writes what he wishes to say. Much of the new number apparatus and use of plastic numerals helps in a similar way to relieve the tensions of trying to write numbers clearly in the first place.

The solving of these practical difficulties often helps a great deal to ease the emotional problems and frustrations from which the child suffers, as he is then able to experience success and also to begin to build up a body of achievement. This in turn, we have found, frequently enables him to accept and also to reveal his other weaknesses and problems.

The teaching of all these children is a constant challenge to the teacher. The new techniques being evolved for helping them and for assessing their needs may result in far-reaching changes in the education of all children, for in the attempts to solve the problems which their education presents, we are learning much more about learning processes in general, and the ways in which to apply this knowledge to increase achievement. Perhaps in another way, we may also learn both as parents and teachers from our increased knowledge of these different problems to suspend judgement and to get fuller information before deciding a child is just 'lazy', 'clumsy', 'babyish' or plain 'awkward and stubborn'. Peter, for example, nearly revolted permanently against school and learning because a despairing teacher tied him to his chair in order to 'make him sit still and learn'. He needed help to overcome his difficulties, and now is a full-time member of a normal school. It is extremely improbable that he is a unique case.

Chapter Eleven
Children with Language Difficulties

Severe reading retardation

'Speech plays a vital part in the organization of complex forms of mental activity.'[1] Since this statement is now generally accepted, it follows that any child who is slow in acquiring and developing speech is likely to be retarded in other ways. Some children do not speak because they are deaf in some degree or other. Nowadays the majority of these children are identified at the baby and welfare clinics or by the health visitors, and remedial education techniques are usually begun by the time they are two and a half years old, if not sooner. Other children who do not communicate verbally may be psychotic or severely subnormal and have already been discussed in this book. In addition to these, there are a few children (202 in all in January 1965) who suffer from such severe speech disorders and defects that they need continuous training and treatment, and whose disorders are known to be due to either:

1. Organic defects of the central nervous system which are frequently congenital;

2. Various forms of aphasia which may be either congenital or developmental in origin, or the result of head injury; or

3. Functional or mechanical defects such as cleft palates.

On the whole these children go to special boarding schools, such as Moor House in Surrey which was set up and is financed by the Invalid Children's Aid Association or the John Horniman School at Worthing. In these schools the emphasis is on continuous speech therapy which often involves play therapy. In school the bulk of the children's activities are also directed towards the development of language skill. The work of the speech therapists, teachers and housemothers who care for the children out of school, is planned as a whole and is completely geared to help the children to overcome their severe handicap.

When all these groups have been put upon one side, there still remains a group of children who appear to comprehend speech but who are not talking at three or even later. Since some of these do begin to talk eventually without remedial teaching, it has been widely accepted that such children are 'slow developers' (whatever that may mean in this context) and many anxious mothers have been advised in consequence to wait, 'stimulate the child verbally', and all will be well! It is now much more widely appreciated that late development of speech should not be accepted in this way, for it may have far-reaching consequences even if the child does begin to talk ultimately. Recently a series of epidemiological inquiries were carried out on all the children living on the Isle of Wight who were born during the two years September 1953 to August 1955.[2] Some of the findings of this survey will be discussed later in this chapter. For the moment it is interesting to note that a significant number of the children who were severely retarded in reading, although of average intelligence, were in fact backward in developing speech and still displayed immaturities of speech at ages nine and ten. A large proportion of them used less complex speech than is normal at that age and one in six of the backward readers showed subnormalities of articulation. Since these children were also backward in mechanical arithmetic and spelling, the findings do provide supportive evidence of the stated effects of delayed speech on mental activity.

At present we are still only beginning to recognize this problem as a problem and to postulate hypotheses as to its aetiology. Some of the recorded observations, such as the fact that there are many more boys than girls, suggests that a genetic factor may be involved. Undoubtedly also among these children there will be some with cerebral lesions and dysfunctions. There are others with no neurological evidence of such defects. Kinsbourne[3] makes the interesting suggestion that in some of these cases the relevant brain areas may have failed to develop at the normal rate because of a chemical failure. He writes:

For example, it may be that even in the very young organisms, certain brain cells are 'predestined' to become involved in language processes.

This would imply that they are distinguished by some 'label' presumably of a chemical nature, some chemical compound they do not share with other brain cells. Now if the reactions that produce this chemical fail, the cells remain unlabelled and do not function as expected. Alternatively the reaction may be too fast, or if waste products are not sufficiently rapidly removed they may poison the cells with similar consequences.

He goes on to point out that 'these are hypothetical mechanisms, but something along these lines quite probably occurs.'

An interesting finding was reported by Stark.[4] He investigated the developmental histories of thirty-three non-verbal children aged between three years nine months and nine years three months whose 'language difficulties were presumed to be on the basis of some possibility of central nervous system dysfunction.' These children were seen at the Scottish Rite Institute for Childhood Aphasia, Stanford University School of Medicine, and were given a very comprehensive examination which included 'medical, audiological, psychological, speech and language studies'. Among the children was a group of twelve who had marked behavioural aberrations and autistic manifestations. The thirty-three children were therefore considered as two separate groups and their deviations on six variables were listed and compared. These were:

1. Early history of poor feeding habits;
2. Limited babbling and generally quiet during prelingual period;
3. Delayed onset of first words;
4. Delayed development of gross motor skill;
5. Mild hearing loss;
6. EEG abnormality.

The only variable which proved to be statistically significant between the two groups was that a far higher proportion of the children in the second group (i.e. those who did not display behaviour disturbances) had an early history of poor feeding habits. The suggestion is made that 'the child who has had considerable discomfort in feeding may not be inclined to derive much satisfaction from additional oral activities'. These children were probably a highly selected group since a high proportion of EEG abnormalities (unspecified unfortunately) was found in both groups of children.

The suggestions made both by Kinsbourne and Stark typify the many areas in which research into this problem needs to be undertaken. If early positive attempts to stimulate a child to speak are successful, both the emotional stresses and anxieties of the parents and the children will be reduced and also the possibility of their later retardation in educational achievement. For this it is necessary that the all too common attitude of *laissez-faire* be altered, as must also a too facile conclusion that a speechless child of three-plus is necessarily severely subnormal. Green reports on the successful outcome of individual speech therapy intensively applied in some cases.[5] She also mentions the role that the mother can be trained and helped to play a part in furthering and assisting in the work of the speech therapist. Ideally it would probably be best if all of these children could be given individual speech therapy, although this may prove impossible to achieve in practice at present, simply because not enough speech therapists are available. Since, however, the intelligent and willing mother is well able to help give the child the constant practice he needs, it might be possible for the speech therapists who are available to maintain an over-all control but to help more children by guiding the mothers to play a larger role in the actual carefully designed play therapy and constant speech and 'babble' development and stimulation which, according to Green, can sometimes be successful. If, for one reason or another, the mother cannot undertake this task, these children could be given high priority in whatever nursery-school facilities are available in the neighbourhood, and the nursery-school teachers could be guided to help in a similar way. This would be necessary since, as Green points out, unless special care is taken an ordinary nursery school may be too stimulating and advanced in its demands for the non-verbal child and therefore he might tend to withdraw further and so have his initial problems exacerbated.

Although from the findings of the Isle of Wight survey which have so far been reported by Dr Rutter and his colleagues in various papers, it appears that a proportion of the children who are very retarded in reading have been late in developing speech and language, and also have a familial history of late language development, this is not the case with all children who are backward readers, since normal language development is not the only pre-requisite for reading competence.

A child also needs to be able to recall and recognize the spatial aspects of visual forms. He has to be able to remember the direction in which individual letters face and the order of letters in a given word. In addition his eyes need to move consistently from left to right. ... Inadequate eye movements ... could limit the child's reading rate but impaired recollection of orientation and sequences can have more serious consequences.[3]

Dyslexia

Unfortunately, perhaps, a new 'label' – dyslexia – is coming into common use to describe collectively children with severe reading difficulties. Dyslexia by itself simply means an impairment of the ability to comprehend and interpret the written word. Used loosely as if it identified a specific handicap it is as inaccurate and useless a label as 'brain damage'. In fact there is no general agreement as to what is meant even by the concept of 'specific dyslexia' or, as it is sometimes called, 'word blindness'. This is partly because, as Dr Rutter and his associates in the Isle of Wight survey point out, most of the reported investigations have been concerned with highly selected groups of children, and therefore the findings depend in part upon the speciality of the investigator. Children who are backward in reading can be reasonably and legitimately referred for investigation to such different specialists as neurologists, child psychiatrists, remedial teachers, speech therapists or educational psychologists, and the referral will depend upon the postulated diagnosis and bias of the person who has made it. The great advantages of a total population survey such as the Isle of Wight are that they avoid the limiting factors of these kinds of biases; they enable planning of special services to be based on a knowledge of the actual size of the problem and the nature of the difficulties found; and by a global examination of the problems found they provide information on the nature of the conditions and the factors with which they are each associated. Such a survey could therefore establish whether there are educational problems such as 'specific dyslexia' which are different from the rest.

The following are the findings of the Isle of Wight survey with regard to the children with severe reading retardation which meant in this context that they were at least twenty-eight months backward in reading. It was found that one child in twenty-five showed this degree of backwardness. In addition, there were many others who, although not so severely retarded, were still backward enough to be handicapped in school. Of the severely retarded readers, 76·7 per cent were boys. The social background of all these children was close to normal and they were of average intelligence. Nearly a quarter of the children who were found to be maladjusted or to be suffering from epilepsy or a neurological disorder were also backward readers, but it was found that it was the anti-social maladjusted children and not the neurotic children who were so retarded.

On detailed investigation of the backward readers it was found that the children were also markedly retarded in spelling and mechanical arithmetic. No association was found between reading difficulties and inconsistent hand preference, although compared with the general population more of the backward readers had difficulties differentiating right from left. Although previous research had suggested that there might be a connection between that kind of muscle twitching called 'choreiform movements' and reading difficulties, no such association was found in this survey. However, many of the backward readers were found to be clumsy in their movements and to have difficulties in copying geometric shapes and in making them with matches. Although other researchers have found that any discrepancy between verbal and performance scores on the WISC intelligence battery has been associated with reading retardation, in this survey such an association was only found when the child's scores on the performance tests were significantly higher than those on the verbal tests. This did seem to indicate that, at least, reading difficulties were strongly associated with an over-all language problem in spite of the fact that some of the children also had spatial problems. The late speech development of a significantly large proportion of the children has already been mentioned. It was also found that in over a third of the group at least one other member of the child's immediate family had had reading difficulties. This could be evidence in favour of a hereditary difficulty but, as Dr Rutter and his associates point out, it is not conclusive since parents who do not themselves read early and with enjoyment or who have had language difficulties may not, either through custom or choice, provide an environment which would positively stimulate the child to develop in these ways.

The strong association between reading difficulties and anti-social behaviour is interesting, but perhaps not unexpected in itself. However, when studied in conjunction with the incidence of speech abnormalities and clumsiness in the non-maladjusted and the maladjusted backward readers, the difference between the two groups is not significant. This means that more research will be needed to study the possibilities which arise from the finding that either the reading backwardness could be a product of the anti-social behaviour or the anti-social behaviour is a consequence of the reading retardation or, and this is the most probable, that both the anti-social behaviour and the reading retardation may be due to other factors entirely.

The findings of this survey have, as was hoped, thrown some light upon the concept of specific dyslexia as a developmental disorder, either constitutional or genetic in origin. Specific dyslexia is usually described as being associated with a family history of reading backwardness, speech difficulties, clumsiness, poor right–left differentiation, poor spelling and defects in spatial concepts. Although, considered separately, all of these factors were found to be associated with reading disability, most of them were only found to be so associated in a minority of cases, and the incidence of some of them did not differ to any significant extent from that found in the normal population. Of even more importance when evaluating the concept of specific dyslexia based upon the factors mentioned, it was found that they did not group together in any significant way. The evidence of this survey is therefore clearly against there being a unique syndrome of specific dyslexia.

Further research and the more detailed analysis of the findings of this survey may show that there are several distinct types of 'specific dyslexia'. On the other hand no specific syndromes may be found. What has been clearly established is the importance of the developmental or constitutional factors in the child, associated with language, motor and perceptual functioning.

The findings of this survey suggest that early identification and follow-up studies of children 'at risk' to develop reading difficulties would not only help the particular children, but would also enable more accurate information on the problem as a whole to be collected. The children who, at five, are delayed in speech, or clumsy, or who show disturbed anti-social behaviour are the ones who should be considered. Until this research has been done we cannot make general statements, for we do not know at present why some children who are severely retarded in reading are clumsy, and others are not, nor why some clumsy children can read well, and others very badly. The same applies to all the other factors which are frequently held to be associated with 'specific dyslexia'.

Important though the findings of this survey are, since they are based upon a total population, it should be emphasized that they are in no way claimed to be conclusive. The Isle of Wight was selected for investigation since it displays in miniature areas where the social class distribution is similar to that of the country as a whole, and where over three-quarters of the inhabitants live in urban areas as designated by the Registrar-General's criteria. It is also an area which has well-integrated education, health and children's services provided by a single local authority, and which compares well with other local authorities in its provision of services. A replication of the survey in other areas would obviously be of tremendous over-all value.

The extent of the need for special provision has been revealed in the survey which has also shown the inadequacies of the present amount of remedial provision. For example, although ninety-two children were thought to need psychiatric treatment, only seventeen were receiving it. The total number of children found to be severely retarded in reading was eighty-eight and of these, at the time of the survey, only eleven were being helped in special classes and another eleven in a special day school for slow learners. Subsequently, eight more were given special help. Since, as has been said, the Isle of Wight does compare well with most other authorities in its provision of special educational services, these figures are probably representative of those which would be found if other authorities were to be investigated in the same comprehensive way. Much greater provision is obviously needed and also much more experimental investigation both of the underlying reasons for the children's difficulties and also of the most effective type of special educational treatment.

There has possibly been more research into different methods of teaching reading than in any other field, but the evidence is by no means conclusive as yet with regard to any of them. It does seem as if these researches are very prone to be influenced by the 'Hawthorne' effect; that is to say, the results which at first appear to be the consequence of the techniques used are in fact much more often found to be due to the feelings of personal interest and official approval felt by all of those taking part in the experiment. The results of some of the researches into phonic techniques and i.t.a. (initial teaching alphabet) have both been shown to be affected by this. In fact there is still a great deal of debate and conflicting evidence as to the results achieved by the use of i.t.a. Unfortunately, the official evaluation of the experiment is proceeding much more slowly than was hoped. Whatever its ultimate merits may prove to be, it is clearly debatable whether it would ever be a good technique to use with the group of backward readers who have gross difficulties in spelling. The findings of an investigation by Jones of the London University Institute of Education favour the use of colour-story reading, in which colour is used both as an aid to identifying words and to convey additional phonetic information.[6] Children taught in this way were found to be about fourteen months ahead of the control groups at the end of their second year. In some of the tests in this experiment the i.t.a. groups were worse than the control groups but were one month ahead of them on the Schonell Graded Word Reading Test at the beginning of the third year.

Perhaps the questions will only be resolved when attempts to teach the children by different techniques are combined with knowledge of the child's learning characteristics, as described in the previous chapter. It would seem logical when children of normal intelligence have failed to learn to read by the usual methods, all of which are largely visual in their approach, to exploit a more preferred sensory pathway to aid the child's appreciation and understanding. I have wondered whether the extreme cases of the children who are so seriously handicapped in visual reading that they never achieve a reasonable standard, might not do better if they were taught to read in Braille. The fact that many more 'taped' books are now available and that tape-recorders are more commonly available may also provide another answer to the problem as to how these children can achieve their full potential.

Meanwhile, since there is no general agreement as to what the symptoms which constitute a syndrome of 'specific dyslexia are, and since the findings of the Isle of Wight survey do not support the suggestion that there is a significant grouping together of the factors usually described as being connected with it, it might be better at present to drop the use of the term as a diagnostic or collective label. It has no value and can lead to misunderstanding and distress between the parents and different specialists, local education authorities and also to the advertising of certain techniques as a 'cure' long before we have sufficient knowledge even of the condition let alone the remedies to justify any such claim.

Conversely it may be dangerous in the opposite direction if the label is applied and the condition regarded as irremediable. Surveys have shown that even if such a condition does exist it is extremely rare indeed, therefore in all cases of reading retardation it is far better to attempt both to analyse the reasons for the failure and to use the utmost ingenuity to find ways and means to overcome it.

Chapter Twelve
Conclusion

I have attempted in this book to examine the needs of children who for one reason or another do not function on the same intellectual and educational level as do normal children of the same age. The possible reasons for their handicaps have been discussed in those cases where they are known and the provision which is made to help the children has been explored. In covering such a wide field many things have had either to be omitted or to be discussed with a brevity which conceals their importance. Among these is the contribution which is made by all the various privately financed schools and institutions, such as the Rudolf Steiner schools and the Ravenswood Foundation, the Home Farm Trust and increasing number of CARE villages founded and inspired by Peter Forbes which are demonstrating in the most remarkable way both how possible it is practically and financially to provide admirable homes for the severely subnormal or socially inadequate adult and how they improve in every possible way when they are members of a community in which they all have an active, interesting and profitable role allotted to them according to their ability. The main reason for this was that I wished to concentrate upon the provisions made by the community as a whole, through the various government departments, local authorities and regional hospital boards. These children and their parents form part of our society and therefore it is the responsibility of us all, as members of the same community, to see that they are both accepted as such and that their needs are adequately supplied from our common resources.

A large share of the credit for the advancement of knowledge and improvement of services which have undoubtedly been made in this century is due to the work done by the different voluntary societies, many of which were in fact created by the parents of handicapped children. Many of the projects and reforms which they initiated have now become incorporated into the community services. This invaluable work is still in progress and cannot be overestimated. However, it does seem to me to be subject to one danger and that is the occasional tendency of some of the leaders of the smaller societies to become so deeply involved in providing in their own way for the special needs of the children in whom they are interested that they generalize too completely from their own private knowledge of one or two children. This can lead to premature statements both as to the aetiology of a condition and the best methods of treating and educating all children who suffer from the same condition. This is not to say that educationalists have nothing to learn from the experiences of these parents – the reverse is true – but teachers and other therapists do have the undoubted advantage of professional expertise and also of being free from the deep personal involvement of the parents. It is often difficult enough for a teacher to distinguish whether it is the techniques which he or she is employing or his or her relationship with the children which is the initial cause of any successes they achieve. It would be extremely difficult for a parent, no matter how professionally trained and skilled in any other direction, to achieve the necessary detachment.

Certain basic themes have appeared in every section of the book: one is the need for more research into every aspect of the subjects discussed and the inadequacy of the financial provision which is made for it at present. At the very least, this is economically unsound because if by medical research the pathological incidence of mental deficiency can be drastically reduced, as seems possible from the evidence which does exist, the amount of provision which needs to be made will be automatically reduced by the same extent. Similarly, if social and educational research leads to increased efficiency in the service provided, many more children and families as a whole will be helped to be self-supporting, or at least enabled to support themselves in part.

Another theme is the beneficial effect of true community acceptance of the mentally handicapped, coupled with an actual personal involvement. Two examples of this have been discussed.

One was the dramatic improvement found in the severely sub-normal hospitalized children who took part in the research project conducted by Stephen and Robertson,[1] when in the final year of the experiment, volunteers from the neighbourhood took a personal interest in the children and widened all their experiences by taking them out of the hospital and into the world outside. The other was the improvements in the severely sub-normal adults in the sheltered workshop at Brighton, when the employees in the other firms in the building both accepted them and demonstrated their acceptance.

The reverse is, unfortunately, also true. As long as children and adults become inmates in institutions because there is nowhere else for them to go or because their families have had to give up the struggle to contain them, as long as it is virtually impossible to obtain permission to set up provision for the mentally handicapped without a protracted struggle, we cannot claim that there is true acceptance of the mentally handicapped into and by the community. A survey of a random selection of local papers will almost inevitably produce evidence of the fact that prejudice still exists. For example, the headline story in a local paper on 5 June 1968 read 'Seven-year wait ends: but site for "School" worries parents'. For seven years a scheme to provide the first centre for severely subnormal children in a prosperous urban area near London had been in the pipeline, and now it seemed that one of the reasons why it might finally be approved was that the site upon which it was to be built was in a road that was due to be cut in two when a new motorway was built; it would then no longer be suitable for residential purposes because of noise. In fairness it should be said that the proposed building would have been well designed for its purpose and to withstand noise from the motorway. However, it is not surprising that parents were worried by the location of the site, although their pathetic conclusion that 'even an inconvenient site is better than none' is understandable in the circumstances. A subsequent edition of the paper, that of 19 June 1968, reported that the Finance Committee of the County Council concerned had voted to shelve the plan yet again, along with three others designed to provide for the mentally handicapped, because of 'the economic climate'. The total cost of the schemes – £307,000. Thanks to the persistence of some members of the committee this decision was later rescinded and the plans re-approved.

Although the situation has improved recently, it is still far from unusual to find similar examples. In 1971 there was nearly a local 'war' when plans to site a hostel in a certain street were bitterly opposed by all the residents purely on the grounds that the residents in a nearby street of large detached houses had successfully opposed having the hostel in their road. It is still a major problem to get planning permission to use any site or existing premises as a school or hostel for the mentally handicapped or ill. Even in the Wessex region which has successfully set up new hostels three out of five are on hospital sites, one on a local authority site and one only in a residential area.

Another main theme which has consistently emerged is the vital importance of the early years in the life of the child, both for diagnosis and prognosis. We cannot adopt the attitude towards a child who is under-functioning in any respect, that we should 'wait and see'. No harm can ever be done by investigating and then attempting to supply a need if it is found to exist, whereas the consequences of not doing so may prove to be irreparable.

Much has been achieved but there is still a great deal of inequality of provision in the various parts of the country. Too often the amount and kind of help a child receives depends not upon his needs, but upon what is available in the area where he happens to live. The methods of ascertainment show a great deal of variation and also the means of identifying at an early age all children in need of detailed investigation.

A great deal of the special education which is given takes place, in theory, in special classes in the normal schools; yet there is very little information both as to the true amount of real provision which is made in this way and also of its efficiency. The results of the survey discussed indicate that in secondary schools at best it falls far short of being satisfactory in every way. Too much also still seems to depend very much upon where a child happens to live. These special classes are also highly vulnerable to every form of shortage in the staffing, accommodation and other facilities in the school. The parent has an undisputed right to consultation and information whenever special education is deemed to be necessary for a child. It is well-established that the interests of a child are the main consideration of the other people involved, namely the teachers, the medical officers and the local authorities upon whom the responsibility of providing it rests. Sometimes, however, problems arise because of a breakdown in communication between the parents and the local education authority. Examples of this also frequently appear in the press: one of the Sunday papers, in March 1968, quoted the case of a child of ten who was not able to read. Her parents were, understandably, deeply concerned and the evidence was that the local authority had also been concerned and had made considerable efforts to find a suitable special school for the child. Unfortunately, however, they had not fully informed the father of the type of school to which she was sent. The reason given when the case went to court was that 'a formal notice often frightens the parents'. In some cases this may be true, nevertheless the answer should not be that they are not told, but that a way to tell them which is not frightening should be found. Over and over again, a formal notice appears to be all that is sent, both when a decision is made to send a child to a special school, but also, and this sometimes causes even more distress, when their child is to be excluded from a special school which they have accepted because it has not proved to be the right one for one reason or another. It does seem also that the assumption is too frequently made that parents need shielding from the true facts. At a recent lecture techniques for helping young blind children were being described, and the statement was made that the parents didn't need to be told that certain exercises were important but encouraged to play them 'as a game'. In a few cases this might be a true psychological assessment, but the majority of parents ought surely to be regarded as the persons who most need and deserve to be fully informed both as to what is being proposed and also about what it is important to do for the child, and why. This applies most significantly and poignantly right at the beginning when, if their child is severely subnormal, they should both be informed of the facts as far as they are known and at the same time given the maximum support and assistance, both with the immediate problem and their own and the family's reaction to it. That these weaknesses of communication all along the line still exist was only too obvious when I was gathering information for this revised edition. Local authorities who tried to ease the transfer of educational responsibility were severely handicapped in their efforts to do so by the relative lateness of official directives to them. Some of the schools in turn seem to have failed to discuss the matter with the parents. Only too typical were the comments of one parent. 'I feel it is the duty of the local education authorities and head teacher of the school to inform parents of intended changes. The liaison at present is poor.'

The accepted values of organized society towards these children and their parents are revealed by our attitudes towards them as reflected by the acceptance we show to the children, the place we allot them in our society and the actual positive and continuing support, advice and practical assistance which we provide for the parents and the family as a whole. In some essential ways the whole situation has radically altered for the better in the last year. Practical assistance in the form of the 'Constant Attendance Grant' is being given to the families of the most severely handicapped who continue to care for their handicapped member at home. The majority however are still ineligible for such a grant. The hospital and hostel services are planned to be totally reorganized, the difficulty here is the time which is bound to elapse before this is completed even at the most hopeful estimate. The task is to keep the urgency in the situation. That it is terribly necessary was shown by two recent reports, the first of three women who spent more than fifty years of their lives in a mental hospital purely because they had had illegitimate babies and so were deemed to be morally defective, the second of a survey which showed that a third of the long stay patients (130 people) in a mental hospital were quite fit to leave the hospital if only there was somewhere for them to go, the extra tragedy being that after their long stay in the hospital the world is too bewildering for them to live in it without supervision and support.

A very important step forward was the transfer of responsibility for the education of the severely subnormal children to the Department of Education and Science; here again it is necessary to be vigilant to ensure that all urgency is preserved to fully implement the upgrading of the schools so that the provision they make is in every way of equal quality and status to that provided in all other schools.

At present the children who are in the schools for slow-learners are still in a happier position. Not only are they less intrinsically limited but also their schools have been fully functioning for a much longer period.

However, the immediate preparation for the post-school life of the children and the provision of continuing support in their first years in employment is often very inadequate. Although in general these children are integrated into society on a reasonable level of acceptance, they do tend to be the first victims of any economic crisis which enforces redundancy and produces unemployment. If in these circumstances they are left without anyone who knows them to turn to, they are at risk of falling away from social integration and becoming either delinquent or incompetent.

With the growing refinement of diagnostic techniques and increased sophistication of observation, more groups of children are being identified as having symptoms in common, and special educational provision is beginning to be made for them. All such provision is still in the early experimental stages. It may well be the case that soon the whole method of categorizing children for special education will be revised and based not upon their disease or defect but upon their learning characteristics as well as their immediate level of intellectual and emotional functioning. The insights gained by attempting to help these special children and the new techniques based upon the increased knowledge which result, will have much wider application since these children do not differ in kind from all other children, but display in varying degrees of severity all the difficulties and problems faced by the normal child.

Although there is a need for more special schools and centres to be purpose-designed and built, of more radical importance is the growing problem of providing suitably trained teachers in sufficient numbers. Possibly the problem will only be resolved when the value which is put upon education is re-assessed by the community and reflected in revised salaries and status accorded to teachers.

As Pope says, ''Tis education forms the common mind.' To

teach is both a challenge and a privilege. This is perhaps especially true in the field of special education where so much is still unknown and where there is such a lot to be gained in every way from the study of and subsequent attempts to supply the needs of our handicapped children.

References

Chapter One

1. Des Wilson, *Back to School from a Holiday in the Slums,* issued by Shelter, September 1967.

Chapter Two

1. Circular 15/70 to Local Education Authorities and certain other bodies from Department of Education and Science. The Education (Handicapped Children) Act 1970, Section 2.

2. *Their Right to Learn and Live,* published by the National Society for Autistic Children.

3. *International Medical Tribune of Britain,* Medical Tribune Ltd, 28 April 1966, p. 67.

4. P. Mittler, *The Mental Health Services,* Fabian Research Series, no. 252, 1954, p. 20.

Chapter Three

1. *Children in Hospitals for the Subnormal,* Report of the British Psychological Society, 1966.

2. J. Tizard and J. C. Grad, *The Mentally Handicapped and their Families,* Maudsley Monograph, OUP, 1961.

3. *The Needs of Mentally Handicapped Children,* Report of the National Society for Mentally Handicapped Children, 1962.

4. A. Kushlick, 'A community service for the mentally subnormal', *Soc. Psychiat.,* vol. 1 (1966), no. 2, pp. 73–82.

5. H. C. Gunzburg, *Junior Training Centres,* National Association for Mental Health, 1963.

6. B. Kiernan and P. G. Cashman, *A Curriculum Guide for Special Class Teachers,* Commonwealth of Massachusetts Department of Education, 1958.

7. J. Tizard, *Care and Treatment of Subnormal Children in Residential Institutions,* Association for Special Education, 1966.

8. *Evaluating Residential Services for the Mentally Handicapped*, November 1971, Albert Kushlick, M.D., B. ch., M.R.C.P., D.P.M., and *Action for the Retarded, The Field for Residential Care*, September 1971, also by Albert Kushlick.

9. *Better Services for the Mentally Handicapped*, Command 4683, June 1971, Department of Health and Social Security, HMSO.

10. Anne and A. D. B. Clark, *Mental Deficiency – The Changing Outlook*, Methuen, 1963.

11. *Quarterly Series*, no. 5, Yorkshire Region of NSMHC.

Chapter Four

1. A. Hargrove, *Serving the Mentally Handicapped*, NAMH, 1967.

2. Department of Education and Science, Circular 15/70

3. *The Challenge of Change*, National Society for Mentally Handicapped Children, Annual Report 1971, p. 4.

4. Joyce McCarthy, 'A change of attitude', *Parents Voice*, vol. 22, no. 1, March 1972, p. 4.

5. L. C. Pryar, 'The end of isolation', *Parents Voice*, vol. 22, no. 1, March 1972, p. 5.

6. P. F. Simpson, 'Training centres – a challenge', *spec. Educ.*, vol. 56 (1967), no 3, pp. 4–8.

7. D. Norris, 'The retarded child at school', *Proceedings of the European Congress of the Education and Training of the Mentally Handicapped*, European League of Societies for the Mentally Handicapped, 1961.

8. A. Marshall, *The Abilities and Attainments of Children Leaving Junior Training Centres*, NAMH, 1967.

9. N. O'Connor and B. Hermelin, *Speech and Thought in Severe Subnormality*, Pergamon Press, 1963.

10. H. C. Gunzburg, *Senior Training Centres*, Subnormality Series, no. 3, NAMH, 1963.

Chapter Five

1. *Special Education Treatment*, pamphlet no. 5, HMSO, 1946.

2. *Statistics of Education*, vol. 1 (1970), England and Wales, p. 56.

3. *Educating our Handicapped Children*, Working Party Report on Special Education, Confederation for the Advancement of State Education, 1966–7.

4. *Slow Learners at School*, education pamphlet no. 46, Department of Education and Science, HMSO, 1964.

Chapter Six

1. *Report of a Survey of Deaf Children who have been transferred from Special Schools to Ordinary Schools*, Ministry of Education, HMSO, 1963.

2. *Slow Learners in Secondary Schools*, Department of Education and Science, Survey 15, HMSO.

Chapter Seven

1. A. E. Tansley, 'Children "at risk" ', *Spec. Educ.*, vol. 55 (1966). no. 1, pp. 15–18.

2. *Slow Learners at School*, education pamphlet no. 46, Department of Education and Science, HMSO, 1964.

3. A. E. Tansley and R. Gulliford, *The Education of Slow-Learning Children*, Routledge & Kegan Paul, 1960.

4. J. J. McCarthy and S. A. Kirk, *Illinois Test of Psycholinguistic Abilities – Examiners' Manual*, Illinois University Press, 1961.

5. 'Too many coloured children still dubbed E.S.N.', *The Times Educational Supplement*, 28 April 1972.

6. N. Jackson, 'How reliable are follow-ups?', *Spec. Educ.*, vol 55 (1966), no. 1, pp. 4–6.

Chapter Nine

1. L. Kanner, 'Early infantile autism', *Child Psychiatry*, C. C. Thomas, 3rd edn, 1944.

2. M. Creek *et al.*, 'Schizophrenic syndrome in children', *Brit. med. J.*, vol. 2 (1961), pp. 889–90.

3. V. Lotter *et el.*, 'Epidemiology of autistic conditions in young children: (1) prevalence', *Soc. Psychiat.*, vol. 1 (1966), no. 3, pp. 124–37.

4. L. Bender, 'Childhood schizophrenia', *Amer. J. Orthopsychiat.*, vol. 17 (1947), p. 40.

5. R. West, *Childhood Aphasia*, Stanford University Press, 1962.

6. B. Rimland, *Infantile Autism*, Methuen, 1965.

7. L. Wing, *Autistic Children*, NAMH, 1964.

8. B. Hermelin and N. O'Connor, 'Sensory dominance in autistic early imbecile children and controls', *Arch. gen. Psychiat.*, vol. 12 (1965), p. 99.

9. S. J. Hutt, C. Hutt, D. Lee and C. Ounsted, 'A behaviour electroencephalographic study of autistic children', *J. psychiat Res.*, vol. 3 (1965), p. 131.

10. Des Lauriers and B. Carlsen, *Your Child Is Asleep*, Dorsey Press, Illinois.

11. A. F. Tredgold and K. Soddy, *Textbook of Mental Deficiency*, Braillier, 10th edn, 1963.

12. L. Goldie and C. van Velzer, 'Innate sleep rhythms', *Brain*, vol. 58 (1965), pp. 1043–56.

13. M. Rutter, 'Schooling and the autistic child', *Spec. Educ.*, vol. 56 (1967), no. 2, pp. 19–25.

14. G. D. Clark, *Some Approaches to Teaching Autistic Children*, Pergamon Press, 1965.

15. M. Lovat, 'Autistic children in a day nursery', p. 12 in Clark (14).

16. P. Mittler, 'Education of psychotic children', p. 26 in Clark (14).

Chapter Ten

1. R. G. Mitchell, 'Minimal disorders of cerebral function', *Brit. J. Disord. Communic.*, vol 1 (1966), no. 2, pp. 109–13.

2. *Isle of Wight Survey* carried out by Prof. J. Tizard and Drs. M. Rutter, K. Whitmore, P. Graham, B. Pless and W. Yule, sponsored by the Department of Education and Science, Association for the Aid of Crippled Children and the Medical Research Council, 1965.

3. K. Wedell, 'Variations in perceptual ability among types of cerebral palsy', *Cerebr. Palsy Bull.*, vol. 2 (1960), no. 3, 1960.

4. See *Children with Cerebral Palsy*, Education Survey 7, Department of Education and Science, HMSO.

5. A. Bowley, 'Studying children from Cheyne', *Spec. Educ.*, vol. 56 (1967), no. 1, pp. 26–9.

6. L. Gardner and J. Johnson, 'The long-term assessment and experimental education of retarded cerebral palsied children'. *Develop. Med. child Neurol.*, vol. 6 (1964), no. 3, pp. 250–60.

7. J. Loring, 'Meldreth: a pioneer unit for the training of spastic children', *Spec. Educ.*, vol. 55 (1966), no. 1, pp. 20–24.

8. E. Marlow, M. Thomas and A. Innes, 'Spastics in ordinary schools', *Spec. Educ.*, vol. 57 (1968), no. 1, pp. 8–13.

9. J. J. McCarthy and S. A. Kirk, *Illinois Test of Psycholinguistic Abilities – Examiners' Manual*, Illinois University Press, 1961.

Chapter Eleven

1. A. R. Luria and P. Yudovitch, *Speech and the Development of Mental Processes in the Child*, Staples Press, 1959; Penguin 1971.

2. *Isle of Wight Survey* – see ref. 2 under Chapter Ten.

3. M. Kinsbourne, 'Backward readers – but why?', *Spec. Educ.*, vol. 55 (1966), no. 3, pp. 23–5.

4. J. Stark, 'A typical development and behaviour in some non-verbal children', *Brit. J. Disord. Communic.*, vol. 2 (1967), no. 2, pp. 146–7.

5. M. C. L. Green, 'Speechless and backward at three', *Brit. J. Disord. Communic.*, vol. 2 (1967), no. 2, pp. 134–45.

6. K. Jones, 'Comparing i.t.a. with colour-story reading', *Educ. Res.*, vol. 10 (1968), no. 3, pp. 226–34.

Conclusion

1. E. Stephen and J. Robertson, paper 4 in *Mental Retardation: Occasional Papers*, 2, 3 and 4. Published by the Butterworth Group for the Institute for Research into Mental Retardation, 1973.